May–August 2023

Day by Day
with
God

Rooting women's lives in the Bible

BRF

15 The Chambers, Vineyard
Abingdon OX14 3FE
brf.org.uk

Bible Reading Fellowship is a charity (233280)
and company limited by guarantee (301324),
registered in England and Wales

ISBN 978 1 80039 177 2
All rights reserved

This edition © 2023 Bible Reading Fellowship
Cover image © Sergii Mostovyi/stock.adobe.com

Distributed in Australia by:
MediaCom Education Inc, PO Box 610, Unley, SA 5061
Tel: 1 800 811 311 | admin@mediacom.org.au

Distributed in New Zealand by:
Scripture Union Wholesale, PO Box 760, Wellington
Tel: 04 385 0421 | suwholesale@clear.net.nz

Acknowledgements
Scripture quotations marked with the following abbreviations are taken from the version
shown. Where no abbreviation is given, the quotation is taken from the same version as
the headline reference. NIV: The Holy Bible, New International Version (Anglicised edition)
copyright © 1979, 1984, 2011 by Biblica. Used by permission of Hodder & Stoughton
Publishers, a Hachette UK company. All rights reserved. 'NIV' is a registered trademark of
Biblica. UK trademark number 1448790. MSG: *The Message*, copyright © 1993, 1994, 1995,
1996, 2000, 2001, 2002 by Eugene H. Peterson. Used by permission of NavPress. All rights
reserved. Represented by Tyndale House Publishers, Inc. NLT: The Holy Bible, New Living
Translation, copyright © 1996, 2004, 2007, 2013. Used by permission of Tyndale House
Publishers, Inc., Carol Stream, Illinois 60188. All rights reserved. NCV: New Century Version®.
Copyright © 2005 by Thomas Nelson. Used by permission. All rights reserved. NRSV: The
New Revised Standard Version of the Bible, Anglicised edition, copyright © 1989, 1995 by
the Division of Christian Education of the National Council of the Churches of Christ in the
United States of America. Used by permission. All rights reserved. AMP: The Amplified® Bible
(AMP), Copyright © 2015 by The Lockman Foundation. Used by permission. **Lockman.org**.
GNT: the Good News Bible published by The Bible Societies/HarperCollins Publishers Ltd, UK
© American Bible Society 1966, 1971, 1976, 1992, used with permission. CEV: Contemporary
English Version © American Bible Society 1995. Anglicisations © British & Foreign Bible
Society 1996. Used by permission. ESV: The Holy Bible, English Standard Version, published
by HarperCollins Publishers, © 2001 Crossway Bibles, a division of Good News Publishers.
Used by permission. All rights reserved. TPT: The Passion Translation®. Copyright ©
2017, 2018, 2020 by Passion & Fire Ministries, Inc. Used by permission. All rights reserved.
thePassionTranslation.com.

A catalogue record for this book is available from the British Library

Printed and bound by Gutenberg Press, Tarxien, Malta

Day by Day
with
God

Edited by **Jackie Harris**   May–August 2023

6   **Jesus is Lord! (Colossians)**
    Alianore Smith
                                                  1–13 May

20 **Lessons from Elijah**
    Selina Stone
                                                  14–27 May

35 **Images for the Holy Spirit**
    Fiona Barnard
                                                  28 May–3 June

43 **What the Bible says about beauty**
    Lyndall Bywater
                                                  4–17 June

58 **Jesus, the healer**
    Lakshmi Jeffreys
                                                  18 June–1 July

73 **Judges: not how things should be**
    Sara Batts-Neale
                                                  2–15 July

88 **How to break the worry habit**
    Bridget Plass
                                                  16–29 July

103 **In the company of trees**
    Jackie Harris
                                                  30 July–5 August

111 **Psalm 119**
    Caroline Fletcher
                                                  6–19 August

126 **God's gift of grace**
    Victoria Byrne
                                                  20–31 August

Writers in this issue

Alianore Smith is church partnerships manager for IJM UK, having previously studied theology at Durham University and worked for the London Institute for Contemporary Christianity. She is author of *Musings of a Clergy Child* (BRF, 2017).

Selina Stone is the postdoctoral research associate at Durham University in theological education. She loves exploring the Bible and Christian faith with a special focus on social justice and concern for those often overlooked in society and the church.

Fiona Barnard is a TEFL/ESOL teacher and staff member of Friends International. She works with international students, encouraging local Christians to reach out in friendship and evangelism to make disciples. She is an honorary chaplain at the University of St Andrews, Scotland.

Lyndall Bywater lives in Canterbury and works with The Salvation Army and the diocese of Canterbury, helping people pray. She is the author of two books, both published by BRF: *Faith in the Making* and *Prayer in the Making*.

Lakshmi Jeffreys began a church placement with Canon David Winter, then editor of *New Daylight*, in 1993. Twenty years later she delighted in seeing her first notes published in the same series. She combines writing with various other roles within and beyond the church.

Sara Batts-Neale is a priest in the diocese of Chelmsford and the Anglican chaplain to the University of Essex. She is married to Tim, and they live with a dog and host a cat.

Bridget Plass is a writer and speaker, appearing and touring with her husband Adrian all over the world. For the past ten years she has enjoyed being actively involved in the programme at Scargill House in Yorkshire and absolutely loves living near Durham.

Caroline Fletcher is a freelance writer with a background in biblical studies. She lives and works in Chesterfield.

Victoria Byrne is married to Tim and leads her church's ministry among older people in Twickenham. She is co-author of *Hope & Spice*, a charity cookbook for Asha Society in Delhi.

Welcome

Some years ago, I was involved in putting together a survey about women and how they read the Bible. One of the questions asked them which books of the Bible were on their most read list and which ones were rarely read. It was interesting to see that some books appeared on both lists – Song of Songs divided opinion, as did Revelation – but there were one or two that were firmly on the rarely read list.

I thought about that when I was talking with a friend about my plans for this issue. When I mentioned I was looking for someone to do a study on the book of Judges, she pulled a face and said: 'Ugh, do you have to do that? Can't you choose something more uplifting?'

Now I am hoping that the majority of studies we do in *Day by Day with God* will be inspirational. In this issue, we will be studying what the Bible says about beauty, focusing on God's grace and Jesus' healing ministry, and learning how to break the worry habit. We'll be encouraged by Elijah, stimulated by Paul's letter to the Colossians and heartened by the work of the Holy Spirit. There is much here to encourage us and build us up in our faith.

But I also believe we need to have a well-rounded knowledge of the Bible. We need to explore all of God's word, for doesn't Paul teach us that 'all Scripture is God-breathed and is useful for teaching, rebuking, correcting and training in righteousness, so that the servant of God may be thoroughly equipped for every good work' (2 Timothy 3:16, NIV)? This challenges me, particularly when I remember that the scripture Paul is referring to is the Old Testament – for the New Testament was yet to be formed. What might we miss if we relegate some parts of the Bible to a rarely read list?

I'm so grateful to Sara who took on the challenge of writing a study on the book of Judges. She not only guides us through this book, but also helps us to think through how we might approach the more challenging parts of the Bible. I hope you will find it as helpful as I did.

Let's begin with some words of a hymn written by Timothy Dudley-Smith: 'Teach us to love the scriptures, Lord, to read and mark and learn; and daily in your written word the living Word discern.' Amen

Jackie Harris, Editor

Jesus is Lord! (Colossians)

Alianore Smith writes:

The title of our study – 'Jesus is Lord!' – is the key message of the book of Colossians. It's a book written by Paul to the Christians in Collosae in AD 60–61. The Colossian church was founded by Epaphrus, one of Paul's converts, and Paul had not yet been able to visit. Letter writing was his only way of communicating with them.

Jesus is Lord! That's the message Paul wants to get across to this church he has loved and prayed for from afar.

Why this in particular? Well, Paul was writing to address the issue of false teaching. False teachers were suggesting that Jesus was not actually God, and so Paul was seeking to bring the Colossian church back to the true gospel of Jesus Christ, God incarnate.

What we will discover as we read this book together – and we're going to read it all over the next fortnight! – is that when we properly understand who Jesus is, every area of our life will be impacted. We will see how Christ is Lord of creation, the church, our salvation and our growth. This has significant implications (as we'll discover in chapter 3) for how we are to live our lives and relate to one another, both as a community and in more personal relationships.

If you take nothing else from the next fortnight, I pray you take this: Christ is our supreme Lord and our sufficient Saviour. When we grasp that truth, and stake our lives on that reality, we will be forever changed.

As we begin this journey together, please join me in praying Paul's words in Colossians 1:9–14, both for ourselves and for all those doing this study alongside us:

May God fill us with the knowledge of his will through all the wisdom and understanding that the Spirit gives, so that we may live a life worthy of the Lord and please him in every way: bearing fruit in every good work, growing in the knowledge of God, being strengthened with all power according to his glorious might so that we may have great endurance and patience, and giving joyful thanks to the Father, who has qualified us to share in the inheritance of his holy people in the kingdom of light. For he has rescued us from the dominion of darkness and brought us into the kingdom of the Son he loves, in whom we have redemption, the forgiveness of sins. Amen

Good fruit

We have heard of your faith in Christ Jesus and of the love you have for all God's people – the faith and love that spring from the hope stored up for you in heaven and about which you have already heard in the true message of the gospel that has come to you. (NIV)

What do you think your church is known for? In the parish or local community, what do people think of when they think of your church? Perhaps you have a thriving youth ministry or a busy food bank. Maybe your church is a piece of architectural brilliance. Perhaps your buildings are known to be cheaper to hire or friendly to drop in to.

The Colossian church was known by Paul for its 'faith in Christ Jesus' and for the love it had for all God's people (v. 4). He had not been able to visit the church, but he had heard of it because of the fruit of their faith, which was the community's love for one another.

This is a letter to a church working out what new life in Christ Jesus looks like. And Paul begins by saying how utterly delighted he is about the fruit of their faith. Because of this fruit – the community's love for one another – he always thanks God when he prays for them.

Before Paul gets into some of the grittier stuff to combat any false teaching, he begins with joy. The gospel is bearing fruit. Hope has given way to faith and love. This is wonderful, wonderful news!

Churches can be known for all kinds of good things: youth ministry, community outreach, beautiful buildings, friendly welcome. They can, of course, be known for negative things as well.

Paul is clear: it is the fruit that we bear as followers of Jesus that shows the truth of the gospel that we believe in. If we have fully heard and 'truly understood God's grace' (v. 6), we too will bear good fruit. May it be so.

Father God, help me to fully understand your grace once again. Remind me afresh of your mighty gospel. And help your church to bear good fruit for your kingdom. Amen

ALIANORE SMITH

Unceasing prayer

For this reason, since the day we heard about you, we have not stopped praying for you. (NIV)

Who do you regularly pray for? Whether family members, specific countries or people groups, friends, colleagues, or godchildren, we all have people for whom we have a specific calling to pray.

As we know, Paul is far away from the church in Colossae, and although he is encouraged by the reports he's hearing of their faith (as we read in 1:1–8), he no doubt felt somewhat helpless when it came to feeding into their discipleship. This wasn't a time when he could shoot off a quick encouraging WhatsApp or get next-day delivery on a handwritten note. This letter – which would have taken a good long while to arrive – was the only means of communication and discipleship he had with them.

And yet.

And yet we see in this letter Paul's declaration that he has 'not stopped praying' (v. 9) for the Colossians. Since the day he heard of their burgeoning faith, he has brought them before the Father in prayer. Paul may not be able to be with the Colossians, but he has a direct line to the God who is, and who has the power to work in and through them for his glory.

Notice also what Paul prays for: knowledge of God's will, bearing fruit for God, strength, endurance, patience and joy. Wouldn't you love to have someone pray these things for you? Wouldn't you love to be able to pray these things for those whom you love?

When we cannot be close to those we love and care for, we can take comfort from the fact that we can talk to the God who *is* close to them and who loves them even more than we do.

Over the next fortnight, as we read through Colossians, commit to praying this prayer (1:9–14) for a different person or group of people each day.

ALIANORE SMITH

What is God like?

The Son is the image of the invisible God, the firstborn over all creation. (NIV)

It's a question which is at once profoundly complicated – theologians have spent thousands of years and millions of words trying to work it out – and yet also deeply simple: just ask a child, and I'm sure they'll tell you.

It's very easy to get caught up in the tangle of what God is or is not like. Although we have the words of the Bible, we also have other people's interpretations of who God is swimming around in our culture. We live in a multireligious society, with many people who have many different ideas of God.

What this passage tells us is simple: if you want to know what God is like, look to Jesus. He – the Son – is 'the image of the invisible God' (v. 15).

It's a bit like this: in the reality TV show *Love Island*, contestants often talk about how someone is 'my type on paper', but when they meet them, things change – they become more or less attractive based on their reality. It's the same with dating apps: you can know a certain amount in theory about a person, but until you meet them properly, you can't truly understand who they are.

This is what Jesus is for God. He is God in flesh – God with skin on. God, walking the earth. Of course, the analogy only extends so far (analogies for the Trinity never quite work!), but the point is this: the more you know about Jesus, the more you will understand about God.

Slowly reread today's passage and consider the impact of the words. What sticks out to you? What surprises you? Thank God for the truth of his word and ask that he would teach you more of who he is.

Father God, thank you for who you are and what you have done in the person of Jesus. Please teach me more of your character today. Amen

ALIANORE SMITH

Hidden treasure

My goal is that they may be encouraged in heart and united in love, so that they may have the full riches of complete understanding, in order that they may know the mystery of God, namely, Christ, in whom are hidden all the treasures of wisdom and knowledge. (NIV)

From *Treasure Island* to *Peter Pan*, we grow up being told stories of pirates and long-lost treasure maps. X marks the spot. That's where the treasure's buried!

If Paul was drawing a treasure map for us in the book of Colossians, the X would be right over the person of Jesus Christ. Paul is not subtle about this, either: 'the mystery of God, namely Christ, in whom are hidden all the treasures of wisdom and knowledge' (2:2–3).

You see, Paul is trying to combat the false teaching of others in Colossae. People have been preaching that wisdom and knowledge – treasure – is to be found elsewhere.

However, rather than beginning with an admonishment or by sending the Colossians on a journey of slowly dismantling any false teaching, Paul is blunt: Jesus is where the treasure is. Anything else will fail to satisfy.

More than that, in fact, Paul is saying that everything the Colossians want to know about God himself can be found in Jesus Christ. Again, that's combatting a false teaching the Colossians were coming up against: that Jesus wasn't truly God. Paul is continuing to bang the drum: Jesus is God. Jesus is Lord. If you want to know who God is, look to Jesus. That's where wisdom and knowledge is.

We live in a world which offers us many suggestions of where wisdom and knowledge can be found. Not all of them are bad, but we face the same challenge as the Colossians did all those years ago: when it comes to our *ultimate* source of wisdom and knowledge, will we look to Christ and Christ alone? Do we truly believe that he alone will satisfy?

Father God, help me to seek all my wisdom and knowledge from things that are of you and you alone. Amen

ALIANORE SMITH

Unshakeable

When you were dead in your sins… God made you alive with Christ. He forgave us all our sins, having cancelled the charge of our legal indebtedness, which stood against us and condemned us; he has taken it away, nailing it to the cross. And having disarmed the powers and authorities, he made a public spectacle of them, triumphing over them by the cross. (NIV)

Do you ever just read a passage of the Bible and get hit afresh by its power? As I read through Colossians, this is one such passage for me.

Paul begins by talking about how we need to *root* ourselves in Christ, remain strong in the faith and continue in thankfulness. If we do that, he says, we will not fall prey to 'hollow and deceptive philosophy' (v. 8). Why? Because when we understand the reality of the God we worship – the one shown in Jesus Christ, who is central and supreme in the universe (1:15–23) – we realise that we do not need to be 'completed' by any other system.

And Paul goes on to explain exactly why. The passage written above is a beautiful summary of the truth of the gospel: we are made alive in Christ. He has taken away all that condemned us. He has nailed it to the cross. And then, even more than that, he took all that wants to harm or rule over us by evil means – 'powers' and 'authorities' – and he triumphed over them as well.

This is huge.

And because of this, we are not bound by – in Paul's words – 'what you eat or drink, or with regard to a religious festival' (v. 16). We are no longer bound by the world's standards; no longer do we have to reach a certain level of righteousness or perfection in order to be accepted. The world's rules are but a shadow (v. 17). The glorious reality is found in Christ… and we are *there*. We 'live our lives in him, rooted and built up in him' (vv. 6–7).

Nothing can shake our foundations in Christ Jesus. Praise God.

Thank you, Father, for the truth of your gospel, poured out afresh on us. May the truth of your grace take root in my life and in my heart, and may I continue to live my life with Christ Jesus as Lord. Amen

ALIANORE SMITH

So what?

Therefore do not let anyone judge you by what you eat or drink, or with regard to a religious festival, a New Moon celebration or a Sabbath day. These are a shadow of the things that were to come; the reality, however, is found in Christ. (NIV)

If ever Paul begins a section with the word 'therefore', it's prudent to glance back quickly at what he's just finished saying. In this case, Paul has just explained the gospel in all its glorious fullness: 'God made you alive with Christ. He forgave us all our sins' (v. 13).

Based on that truth, then, Paul now turns his attention to some of the false teaching the Colossians were battling: people trying to draw them back into rules and regulations.

Paul is particularly concerned that the Colossians do not fall into the same trap that the Galatians had done a few years previously: believing they had to act in a particular way *in order to* earn God's favour and redemption, rather than acting in such a way – as we'll see in Colossians 3 – *because of* their new identity in Christ.

And so Paul is clear: random religious rules and regulations are but a shadow of the reality that is to be found in Christ. When we understand the truth of the gospel, the centrality of Christ and the reality of the identity we now have, everything else should fade into insignificance.

What does this mean for us today? In some ways, it's obvious: we shouldn't be swayed by new-fangled ways to reach new heights of holiness. Nor should we try to convince ourselves that we must act in a certain way in order to be a 'good Christian'. It's not about *trying harder* – in fact, that's the exact opposite of what Paul is saying here! Instead, it comes from letting the truth of the gospel take root in our hearts and letting it change us from the inside out.

Spend some time today dwelling on the truth of the gospel. Ask God to give you faith, and then wonder afresh at his glory and grace.

Thank you, Father, for the sufficiency of your gospel. Thank you that we are no longer bound by what we do but can live in freedom because of what you have done. Remind us of that truth today. Amen

ALIANORE SMITH

A new name

Since, then, you have been raised with Christ, set your hearts on things above, where Christ is… For you died, and your life is now hidden with Christ in God… you have taken off your old self with its practices and have put on the new self, which is being renewed in knowledge in the image of its Creator. (NIV)

When I got married, I decided not only to take my husband's surname (Smith), but also to change my first name from a nickname I'd had for 21 years (Nell) to my given name (Alianore).

Changing my first name meant I had to get used to answering to a name I was only really used to being called when I was in trouble. For a good few months, I had a delayed reaction to being called Alianore because I didn't associate the name with myself. Even though I'd made a decision and asked to be called Alianore, my actions and behaviour showed that I *thought* I was still called Nell.

Paul is writing here about a similar status change. When we become Christians, we are raised with Christ, and our new identity is hidden in Jesus. What is true of Jesus is, suddenly, true of us – and we have to start living as if it were.

Because of this, we need to act in a certain way – we must start answering to a new name, associate ourselves with a new identity. We need to 'put to death' our earthly nature, and instead 'set our hearts on things above' (v. 1).

Often, this will feel difficult. We may not feel like our life 'is now hidden with Christ in God' (v. 3). We may struggle to accept this new reality and act in accordance with it. But, as Tom Wright so beautifully puts it in *Paul for Everyone: The prison letters – Ephesians, Philippians, Colossians and Philemon* (SPCK, 2002), 'learning to believe what doesn't at the moment feel true is an essential part of being a Christian'.

May we trust the truth of God's word, no matter what our feelings or circumstances are telling us.

Father God, help me to trust in you and your truth, in the new identity that you have given me. Help me act in line with my new family name. Amen

ALIANORE SMITH

Love is all you need?

Therefore, as God's chosen people, holy and dearly loved, clothe yourselves with compassion, kindness, humility, gentleness and patience. Bear with each other and forgive one another… Forgive as the Lord forgave you. And over all these virtues put on love, which binds them all together in perfect unity. (NIV)

I once went to a wedding where this passage was read and preached on. During the sermon, the bride and groom were invited up to the front and told to put on various items of clothing – hats, scarves, a jacket – to represent compassion, kindness, humility, etc. This was the clothing they were to wear in their daily lives – both as a couple and among the community.

And then, in an unexpected turn of events, the preacher brought out something else: a pantomime horse. (His name was Horace, in case you were wondering.)

The bride and groom were asked to put on the costume and walk across the front of the church. And so, a little awkwardly, and with plenty of laughs, they did. And they had to do so in sync, walking at the same pace and in the same direction, because they were *bound together* by the pantomime horse.

What was the point of this ridiculous, memorable illustration? You've guessed it: Horace the horse represented the love they were to put on.

Love is what binds together all the other virtues that we are called to put on: compassion, kindness, humility, gentleness, patience, bearing with one another and forgiving each other. These are not just virtues that we must put on in marriage, but in *all* our relationships and in *all* our interactions.

Why? Because we are God's chosen people. We are holy – set apart – and deeply loved. We have been forgiven. And so, we too are called to forgive.

We are in Christ – and so what is true of Christ is true of us. From that position of being God's beloved, and knowledge of it, we can act accordingly. We can put on the (metaphorical) pantomime horse and continue in love for one another.

Father God, teach me to love. Amen

ALIANORE SMITH

All things

And whatever you do, whether in word or deed, do it all in the name of the Lord Jesus, giving thanks to God the Father through him. (NIV)

What's the holiest thing you've ever done? Led someone to faith in Jesus? Read the Bible in a year? Prayed in tongues? Preached?

When we're asked to think of 'holy' things, it's easy to go straight to the usual answers – prayer, evangelism and Bible reading. And don't get me wrong, those are good and holy things to do. But this passage is saying something revolutionary: everything you do matters to God. Everything you do is under the Lordship of Christ. Everything you do – washing up, commuting, changing nappies, planning lessons, battling with spreadsheets – *everything* matters to God.

Our daily lives, in their mundanity and their mania, matter to God. Why do we know that? Well, remember Colossians 1:15–23? Paul is hearkening back to that passage here: if everything is made *through* and *for* Christ, if everything is under his lordship, then everything we do matters to him.

It can be so easy to think that our lives are less spiritually significant if we're not working full-time for a church or a Christian organisation. If, instead, we're working a full-time job in the City, looking after children or laid up at home sick and unable to do much at all, we can think we need to earn more 'Christian points' by leading a church small group or praying harder and more often.

But no, says Paul. *Everything* matters to God. And so, *everything* we do – whether in word or deed – can and should be done to the glory of God.

How would your view of your daily life change if you did it all 'in the name of the Lord Jesus, giving thanks to God the Father through him' (v. 17)? Let me tell you: it revolutionised mine.

Thank you, Father, that you care about every aspect of my life and nothing is too trivial or boring for me to bring to you. Help me to do everything to and for your glory, and may your kingdom come in my work. Amen

ALIANORE SMITH

Living the new life

Wives, submit yourselves to your husbands, as is fitting in the Lord.
Husbands, love your wives and do not be harsh with them. Children,
obey your parents in everything, for this pleases the Lord. Fathers, do
not embitter your children, or they will become discouraged. (NIV)

If you ever find yourself making a speech to an audience with high-profile
guests (think royalty, politicians, archbishops, etc.), you would traditionally
begin by addressing the most important person first: 'Your Royal Highness,
Your Holiness, honoured guests, ladies and gentlemen'.

A similar custom was in place for Roman pagan writers as they wrote
household codes: they would always begin by addressing the person with
the most power. Invariably, that would be the male, the master, the parent.

It is no accident that in Paul's version of the household codes, he does the
opposite. By addressing the less powerful, the 'weaker', the more vulnerable
party first, Paul is making a stark point: there is no hierarchy in Christ Jesus.

Paul has been speaking about wider Christian community. We are living
as those made alive in Christ, in whom there is no favouritism (3:25). We are
putting on love (3:14). And that means things look a little different from what
we might expect – not only for those who are 'weaker', but those afforded
greater worldly power as well.

In addition, Paul is saying to everyone that they have a choice about
how they behave. In a world where stuff was done *to* women, children and
slaves, where authority was imposed on them from above, Paul reminds
us that 'weaker' people have power over their consciences, their motives
and their devotion to Jesus. And the 'stronger' people – the husbands, the
fathers, the masters? They too will be held to account for their actions and
their motives (3:25). This is about treating everyone well – no matter what
power they do or do not hold.

Whatever we do, whether we are wives or children or workers – or different things in different situations – we are doing it all in the name of Jesus,
who has made us all equal in his sacrifice on the cross.

---

*Which part of today's passage do you find most challenging? Bring it before
Jesus and ask him to help you understand it more clearly.*

ALIANORE SMITH

Watching and thanking

Devote yourselves to prayer, being watchful and thankful. (NIV)

How do you pray? Were you taught to pray in a particular way? Perhaps you learnt the 'TSP' method – thank you, sorry, please. Maybe you were brought up with liturgy and set prayers. Or perhaps you go to a church where it's mainly the priest who prays, and you just say 'amen' in agreement.

The Bible shows us that there are many ways to pray: petitions, thanksgiving, repentance, intercession… the list goes on. But here, Paul is asking for prayers for a particular thing, and in a particular way – be watchful and thankful and pray for Paul's message of the gospel.

What do you think it means to be 'watchful' in prayer? It seems that there are many ways of doing so. Perhaps it's about praying protection over people, asking God to watch over them. Or perhaps it means to be particularly aware of your surroundings and situation and praying accordingly. Or maybe it means just taking time to prayerfully understand where God is at work in the world, and joining in. Or it could be something else entirely.

Being thankful is, of course, a much easier one to understand, though not always an easier one to practise. What do you have to be grateful to God for today? Have you managed to vocalise that in prayer?

To pray for the advancement of the gospel is, in some respects, much easier. In others, it is one of the hardest. We can pray generally that God's word would go out, but how can we be praying specifically for those who are called to particular evangelistic ministry? And we must also pray in the knowledge that we are *all* called to share the good news of Jesus and that God has called us to share his gospel with those around us. Let's pray for courage and obedience in that, too.

Father God, teach me how to be watchful and thankful in prayer, and give me the opportunity to proclaim the mystery of Christ to those around me. Amen
ALIANORE SMITH

Keep going

Tell Archippus: 'See to it that you complete the ministry you have received in the Lord.' (NIV)

In Paul's closing reflections, he mentions ten different individuals. Each receives some form of context or introduction or sends greetings to the church in Colossae. Each name has a story behind it. For example, Onesimus (v. 9) is widely assumed to be the same Onesimus in the book of Philemon – a slave on whose behalf Paul pleads. It would be so interesting to learn more about the backgrounds and faith stories of each of these names.

When faced with a list of names such as these, it's easy to skim over them, to see them as irrelevant to our lives today, an epilogue to the letter itself. And yet we know that *all* scripture is God-breathed and useful for us in our discipleship journey (2 Timothy 3:16).

So what is this passage saying to you today? Which individual do you want to learn more about? Whose context or message are you most challenged by?

For me, it's Archippus, for whom Paul has a direct message: 'See to it that you complete the ministry you have received in the Lord' (v. 17). There are so many questions raised by this one short verse. What ministry? Why hasn't he completed it? What does it mean to 'complete' a ministry? Why has he been singled out to receive such specific instructions? So many of these questions go unanswered and will likely remain so… at least until we get to heaven.

We have seen throughout this book Paul's desire to convey the truth that *all* things are under the lordship of Christ, so it's possible that the ministry is not a church-based one. He could have just as likely received a more secular or practical ministry in the Lord. We do not know.

What ministry has the Lord given you? Whether sacred or secular, pray for the strength and perseverance to complete it.

Bring your ministry – or ministries – to God in prayer. Be watchful and thankful alongside him, and pray also for perseverance for others who have been given 'ministries in the Lord'. Amen

ALIANORE SMITH

Remember my chains

I, Paul, write this greeting in my own hand. Remember my chains. Grace be with you. (NIV)

So here we are. Two weeks later and we've read through the entire book of Colossians. And what a journey it's been. Well done!

Today, we conclude by reading the beginning of the book again, along with Paul's closing words. He begins with his standard greeting, but he closes in an unusual way: 'Remember my chains.'

As we know, Paul was writing this letter to the church in Colossae from prison. He had never met these people in person but was writing to combat false teaching of a false gospel, one which argued that Jesus Christ was not God. We have journeyed with Paul through his exploration of the gospel and his conviction that Jesus Christ is central to every part of it, and we've heard him clearly explain the ramifications of this for everyday life and everyday relationships.

There was plenty that Paul could have said to end this letter. But he ends with this: 'Remember my chains.'

I think Paul ended this way because he wanted to remind the Colossians that he was willing to stake his life on what he had written. He was willing to be put in prison, be flogged, be shunned, even be executed, because he so firmly believed that what he had written to them – the truth of the gospel of Jesus Christ – was true.

Are you convinced of this too?

Paul is not the only one who has been in chains for preaching – or simply just believing – the gospel. Over 340 million Christians suffer persecution purely because they confess Jesus Christ as Lord.

Paul asks us to 'remember his chains'. Today, how can we remember our brothers and sisters around the world who wear similar chains for preaching the same gospel?

Take some time to pray for the persecuted church. You can use resources from the Open Doors UK website if that's helpful.

ALIANORE SMITH

Lessons from Elijah

Selina Stone writes:

Elijah is one of the most well-known biblical characters, appearing in both the Old and New Testaments. In the Old Testament, we find thrilling stories of miracles taking place in the homes of widows, rain being held back and a competition with idol worshippers involving bulls and fire from heaven. But under all of this is a real person who struggles with the weight of his calling, and with his fears, insecurities and even suicidal thoughts. We see him at his best when he is calling the people of Israel back to repentance, and at his worst when he gives in to his violent tendencies and they then backfire.

In the New Testament, he reappears as a comparative figure with another prophet – John the Baptist – the one who would prepare the way for Jesus. Elijah then appears to Jesus on a mountain and is believed to have the power to rescue Jesus as he is crucified.

We will consider all these themes and more in the next two weeks, as we trace Elijah's story through the Old and New Testaments. I have intertwined the reflections so that you will be able to see how Elijah's life and ministry has echoed through the ages. It is my hope that as you read these reflections, you will be able to see how his life can inspire and challenge your own.

However, I do not believe that we are all called to be prophets. To me, it is a special ministry of hearing and sharing messages from God which seek to get people back on the right track. It demands a certain level of discernment and courage. But I do believe that as the church – a community of people committed to God – we are called to be prophetic. By this I mean that churches and Christians are called to be 'salt and light' in the world, which includes being prepared to embody and to share the message of Christ and the gospel even when it is unpopular. This includes a willingness to challenge powerful people, institutions, systems and norms which oppose the abundant life Christ has sought to bring us.

May these reflections provoke, inspire and encourage you as you continue to walk with God and seek to share and show the gospel to a watching world.

Divine provision

Elijah went to the Kerith Ravine, east of the Jordan, and stayed there. The ravens brought him bread and meat in the morning and bread and meat in the evening, and he drank from the brook. Some time later the brook dried up because there had been no rain in the land. (NIV)

Elijah's story begins with a prophetic declaration that there will be no rain because God's people refused to uphold their covenant relationship with God. The prophet seeks to get them back on the right path by showing them what life without God's protection and provision is like. Elijah is told to hide in this ravine because king Ahab will hear about Elijah's declaration and seek to kill him. Being a prophet is a dangerous business. But here, God provides what Elijah needs in the form of bread, meat and water each day. Amid a dry time, Elijah has divine sustenance. Ravens, who are known to be scavengers and usually take food away, go against their nature when it comes to Elijah and become instruments of divine provision.

It can be difficult for us to identify with someone like Elijah, who is an unusual character. He makes bold statements to the political leaders of his time and is also homeless and living alone in a secluded ravine where he is fed by birds. He may remind us of people around the world who hide away because of their faith, or risk everything to speak up about what they believe in. But each of us, in our own way, must deal with fear, isolation and insecurity in life. Like Elijah, we too are often in need of divine assistance. We are no less beloved than this prophet, who God knew by name and was sent to a safe place where he would find food and water. Whether we find ourselves alone, waiting in a place we never expected to be or forced to depend on unexpected sources of help, we can trust the God of Elijah to remain close to us, even when the brook dries up.

Lord, we can often struggle to trust you when times are difficult. Please help us to believe that you see us and are guiding us to places of provision, even when we cannot see what lies ahead. Amen

SELINA STONE

Unimaginable prayers

The prayer of a righteous person is powerful and effective. Elijah was a human being, even as we are. He prayed earnestly that it would not rain, and it did not rain on the land for three and a half years. Again he prayed, and the heavens gave rain, and the earth produced its crops. (NIV)

Elijah's famous prayer is so iconic that we see it talked about in the book of James in the New Testament. In teaching the believers about faith and prayer, James uses the example of Elijah, who was just like us and yet was able to stop and start rain due to the power of his prayers. If we are honest, this can be both inspiring and frustrating in equal measure. If we are human just like Elijah, then what goes wrong with our prayers? We might not be praying for anything as significant and complicated as a drought, and yet we might never see the tiniest movement in response to what we are praying for.

I don't think the writer of this letter is trying to give us a detailed formula for Elijah's prayer that we can follow for the same results. But I do think that he is trying to inspire us to pray big prayers, to imagine things we may regard as impossible and to speak boldly. We can often think of prayer as handing over responsibility to God, but in the actual account of the story (in 1 Kings 17:1) it does not say Elijah prayed, but Elijah *said*. We get the impression here that Elijah was so in tune with the mind and the will of God that when he spoke it was perfectly aligned with God's intention. This is the alignment we might pursue as we pray for ourselves, our families, our friends and our communities, and in this we might find a power that we previously have not experienced.

As you reflect on a particular matter which is concerning you, ask God to guide your prayers and your words so that they may align with God's will, and pray earnestly from that place, trusting in the God of Elijah.

SELINA STONE

A poverty miracle

Elijah said to her, 'Don't be afraid… first make a small loaf of bread for me from what you have… For this is what the Lord, the God of Israel, says: "The jar of flour will not be used up and the jug of oil will not run dry until the day the Lord sends rain on the land."' (NIV)

I have always found this story concerning because I grew up in a church tradition where so-called prophets abounded, as did spiritual abuse and manipulation. I remember hearing 'prophets' use the word of God to manipulate women into putting what little they had into the offering basket, promising a return that never materialised.

I have heard this passage used in that exact way. Instinctively, I worry about this widow because she and her son are preparing to die once they have eaten their last little cake, and Elijah is asking her to make one for him first, promising a miracle. I'll be honest: I am the kind of woman who would likely reply, 'Let's see the flour and oil first, then I'll make your small loaf', but women like me don't make for good Bible stories. In this case, she is fortunate that Elijah is not a charlatan, and her act of radical generosity opens up a flood of provision which sustains her and her son beyond that day and into the future.

We are living at a time when life is very precarious for many people. Yet rather than asking the bigger questions about what is happening and why – in this case idolatry and a drought – we are often encouraged to ask questions which inherently blame the victimised person. When we encounter people like this widow, do we empathise with their fears and recognise their agency, or do we view them with suspicion and pity? Elijah provides this woman with oil and flour, but knows the real issue is the drought. He encourages us to recognise the dignity of those with few resources and to acknowledge God's desire to meet their immediate needs and to address the root causes of those needs.

As you pray, consider those people who, like this widow, struggle to live under difficult circumstances beyond their control. What might God lead you to do in the face of their immediate needs and the deeper issues which cause them?

SELINA STONE

Rejected prophets

'Truly I tell you,' [Jesus] continued, 'no prophet is accepted in his hometown. I assure you that there were many widows in Israel in Elijah's time… Yet Elijah was not sent to any of them, but to a widow in Zarephath in the region of Sidon.' (NIV)

As people who are not living at the time of Elijah, there is a certain gap we have to overcome to understand the significance of his words and actions. This is the same for the Jews of Jesus' time, who knew all about the prophets but did not necessarily comprehend them. In this passage, Jesus uses Elijah to make a point about himself: they are both prophets and they have both faced rejection by those they hoped would accept them. Elijah was rejected by the people of Israel and as a result was sent to minister to a widow who was a foreigner. Likewise, Jesus is rejected by the Jews in his hometown, while his ministry thrives among those he meets on his travels.

The question of belonging affects all of us: where do we go when we want to be accepted, be welcomed and feel at home? We may not be rejected because of our prophetic calling, but we might be isolated because we do not fulfil the expectations people have of us. Elijah was expected to be 'normal', to fit in and to go along with the norms of his time, and the same could be said for Jesus. The illusion of the 'normal' can afflict us all. We can feel the pressure to belong by conforming to a 'normal' personality, a 'normal' family, wanting 'normal' things or having 'normal' ambitions. But God called Elijah to be entirely abnormal, and though he was rejected by those he knew, the silver lining was that he was able to care for those who otherwise would have been missed out. Your rejection might in fact turn out to realign you with those things you have not yet imagined, but which God has in mind for you.

As you pray today, bring to God any feelings of rejection or resentment which you may feel and ask God to heal them. In what ways might this realign you with a new sense of calling or belonging?

SELINA STONE

Faithfulness in the small things

'Give me your son,' Elijah replied. He took him from her arms, carried him to the upper room where he was staying... Then he cried out to the Lord, 'Lord my God, have you brought tragedy even on this widow I am staying with, by causing her son to die?' (NIV)

Tragedy can strike when we least expect it, and this is what we are witnessing here. This woman has opened her home to a prophet, which is to open her home to God. Despite this, her son has died, and she is in great distress. I can only imagine her fear and confusion: couldn't the God who prevented the oil and flour running out have prevented her son from dying? I am sure many of us will have asked these questions. Maybe for us it was also the loss of a loved one, or perhaps our own health crisis, the loss of a relationship or of financial security. We can be left with a sense of abandonment and fear.

In this passage, the woman runs to tell Elijah and he responds with great compassion – he shares in her suffering. He does not stand aloof because it is not his child but takes the child in his arms to an upper room and cries out to God for the boy. A story like this can get lost in all the prophetic statements, conversations with kings and national displays of power we will come to later. But it is important to remember that Elijah prays fervently not only to stop or start rain, but also for this little boy who has died.

When we imagine our own lives and our impact in the world, do we value these small moments of compassion and empathy as much as we do the publicly impressive displays of faith? In a world where social media tempts us to focus on impressing others and gaining their approval through big public statements or displays of faith and love, Elijah challenges us to be consistent in the small things and to do them privately.

Thinking about your own prayer life and walk with God, do you struggle to recognise the importance of the small acts of faith? Are you easily moved with compassion for the needs of others? Talk to God about this.

SELINA STONE

Making good trouble

[Ahab] said to [Elijah], 'Is that you, troubler of Israel?' 'I have not made trouble for Israel,' Elijah replied. 'But you and your father's family have. You have abandoned the Lord's commands and have followed the Baals…' Elijah went before the people and said, 'How long will you waver between two opinions?' (NIV)

I was not a troublemaker growing up. It is definitely something I have grown into. As a child, I was a good girl who respected adults, followed the rules and did as I was told. But as an adult, I came to realise that sometimes adults don't know what is happening, the rules do not make sense and doing as you are told can land you in serious trouble or pain. In this conflict between Elijah and Ahab, we see a prime example of this. Ahab sees Elijah as a troublemaker because he is challenging the status quo in which the people of Israel worship idols, betray God and make all the wrong choices about who they should trust. But Elijah is making the best kind of trouble.

As God's prophet, Elijah is being called to agitate those who are used to being comfortable, those who have power and those who are used to doing what they like. He is called to stand up for what is right and to call people back to the right path. I believe the ministry of Elijah challenges us to embrace the troublemaker label – to be those who are, as the American civil rights activist John Lewis (1940–2020) said, 'making good trouble'. This means making trouble for those doing wrong, those mistreating their fellow human beings or those giving worship to things which are not God.

It is also important to remember that at times we will be those people doing wrong and will need someone to make trouble for us. Can we be open to those righteous troublemakers who seek to get us back on the right path?

Lord, thank you for using us to show others the right way and for sending people to do the same for us. Help us to be open to the correction of your Spirit as we go about our lives. Amen

SELINA STONE

The call to turn

'[Your son] will go on before the Lord, in the spirit and power of
Elijah, to turn the hearts of the parents to their children and the
disobedient to the wisdom of the righteous – to make ready a people
prepared for the Lord.' (NIV)

Elijah's ministry appears again in the New Testament, this time as a way of
describing the ministry of John the Baptist. These words are spoken by an
angel to Zechariah while his wife Elizabeth is pregnant with John. It must
have been encouraging for this older couple to hear that the baby they had
longed for was not just an answer to their prayers but would also be an
answer to the needs of the whole world. Elijah is spoken of here as having
a particular 'spirit and power' to restore right relationships and to inspire
people to do what is right in obedience to God.

It is a long time since anyone had to get me ready for anything. I sometimes envy my friend's young children as they are picked up, soothed,
dressed and fed without having to do anything themselves. There is something comforting about this phase of life, but generally we only think that in
hindsight. Children long to grow up so they can prepare themselves, while
many adults long for less to prepare for.

It is interesting that in this passage God not only says preparation is
needed, but he also provides the means for it to happen. Elijah is called
and gifted for this, and the people of Israel only need to receive him. This is
easier said than done in our own lives of course. When God prepares us, it
can feel difficult, especially as we surrender our own will and intentions. But
the sense here is that turning is a necessary part of our formation as Christians, and so is accepting the divine wisdom that leads us to what is right.

---

*As you reflect on the need to turn and embrace the wisdom of God, is their
anyone or anything which helps you to do this? How might you create more
opportunity for this guidance to shape your life?*

SELINA STONE

Temptations of violence

Then the fire of the Lord fell and burned up the sacrifice… When all the people saw this, they fell prostrate and cried, 'The Lord – he is God!'… They seized [the prophets of Baal], and Elijah had them brought down to the Kishon Valley and slaughtered there. (NIV)

All of us can go too far at times, even with the best of intentions, and this to me seems like a prime example. Elijah suggested a competition to prove once and for all that God, not Baal, was the true God. Elijah and the prophets of Baal would prepare the sacrifice and call to their respective deities to answer by sending fire to consume it. God wins the competition, and the people repent and recognise God as the one true God. But Elijah does not stop there; he turns this moment of repentance and worship into one of violence and bloodshed.

Some will defend Elijah by saying he was a man of his time or that it was acceptable because they worshipped other gods. For some readers, this is merely a blip on an otherwise sterling record that we should disregard. To me, this passage warns us of the contradictions we all carry and how moments of glory can reveal the often-hidden evils within us. Elijah calls the people back to God in one breath and in the next slaughters countless numbers of God's children.

We each have to deal with the temptation to harm those we perceive as our enemies and the desire to excuse the many forms of violence we can enact (not necessarily physical). Our calling, though, is to live in alignment with God's best intentions for us, including in terms of how we respond to those we consider 'other': those of other faiths or those we perceive as threats. While we might be tempted to use force to destroy the 'enemy' for perceived good reason, Christ calls us instead to love them.

Take this time to consider those people you might consider to be a threat to you, your family, your faith or your community. Can you bring this to God? What might it mean to resist force and embrace love?

SELINA STONE

On the run

Now Ahab told Jezebel everything Elijah had done… So Jezebel sent a messenger to Elijah to say, 'May the gods deal with me… if by this time tomorrow I do not make your life like that of one of [the prophets of Baal].' Elijah was afraid and ran for his life. (NIV)

Even those of us who generally make wise decisions have, at some point, had to deal with the negative consequences of our actions. For most of us, dealing with those consequences can be as simple as a sincere apology where there was no bad intent. Sometimes it might require significant and costly steps to right a wrong. The most difficult situations I have faced have been when there is nothing that can be done to fix it, and the person is not interested in reconciliation. Elijah finds himself at the most extreme end of this kind of circumstance. Having slaughtered the prophets of Baal in a moment of exuberance, he may now reap the violence he has sown. Jezebel is not open to negotiations, apologies or recompense; she simply wants revenge. And so Elijah runs for his life.

It is interesting to me that Elijah, who has just witnessed the power of God on display, has no confidence that God will look after and protect him if he stays where he is. Does he doubt whether God approved of his actions? Does he imagine that God might let him be killed? We cannot know what was in Elijah's mind, but we can identify with the fear felt when circumstances turn against us and our safety is in question. Maybe we have been our own worst enemy or perhaps we have felt threatened by someone else, but we see in this story that Elijah is protected by God and hidden in a safe place. We can be assured therefore that whatever reason we might be on the run, God is merciful and kind, and he will not deal with us according to our mistakes.

Is there a situation in your own life which causes you to be afraid and has you on the run? Reflect on this and imagine God running alongside you – what might God be saying to you today?

SELINA STONE

Rest in a restless moment

[Elijah] came to a broom bush, sat down under it and prayed that he might die. 'I have had enough, Lord,' he said. 'Take my life; I am no better than my ancestors.' Then he lay down under the bush and fell asleep. (NIV)

We have seen that Elijah's life and ministry is marked by threats of violence, fear and being on the run from those who sought to do him harm. In this passage, we find Elijah at his lowest point. Having run from Jezebel into the wilderness, he is alone, without food or a plan, and wishing to die.

We can sometimes assume that people who lead or take on very demanding roles in the world are a different kind of being to ourselves. I am so familiar with my own inner critic, my doubts and uncertainties, but assume that the people doing great things have none of those battles. Elijah shows us that even the people we might look to as impressive, powerful figures are human beings who need care, struggle with mental health and may at times lose a sense of purpose and self-confidence. They are just like us.

Talking about well-being has become very common now as people have come to realise that, as human beings, our health is essential to a good life, as well as to our productivity. Like Elijah, we can all get so busy fulfilling roles and tasks that we forget to rest and take care of our bodies as well as our souls. We can even slip into thinking that God's love and approval is conditioned by our willingness to accomplish tasks or fulfil a role or our sense of calling. We are not loved more when we are adults because we can do more for God; we are as loved as when we were children doing nothing more than gurgling, sleeping and eating. God's delight in us is eternal, and he invites us to a place of rest and an awareness of our beloved status in him.

Lord, help me to know that I am beloved by you, especially in my lowest moments. Help me to rest in you as I move through my days, and to offer that rest to the weary. Amen

SELINA STONE

Finding community

[Elijah] replied…' I am the only one left, and now they are trying to kill me too.' The Lord said to him…' I reserve seven thousand in Israel – all whose knees have not bowed down to Baal and whose mouths have not kissed him.' (NIV)

I do not know about you, but I can be a little dramatic at times, especially when I am expressing my feelings about something. I might describe something as 'amazing' when it is really just okay, or 'the worst ever' when it is simply mildly annoying. I see a bit of this melodrama in Elijah's words here. This is the second time he has panicked out loud, stating that he is 'the only one left' of the righteous and faithful followers of God. This narrative exacerbates his own anxiety and invokes our empathy as the reader. But here we learn that he is nowhere near correct – in fact, God corrects him, there are 7,000 faithful believers. Elijah is not the only one by a long stretch.

Unbeknown to Elijah, God has been keeping watch over those who believe in him, and Elijah is not, in fact, standing alone among an entire society of idolaters. Though Elijah feels isolated and has been reciting the story of his aloneness, he is in fact part of a community which he could not see. This can be an encouragement to us at a time when social isolation is such a common reality for many people. We should not deny the reality of loneliness: we have so many elderly people living alone, and people of all ages who lack close loving connections. And while people are more connected by technology, it neither prevents nor solves loneliness. But this passage invites us to imagine that the potential for community might not be as far away as we think – in fact, it might be all around us. With God's perspective, we might find people of like mind right under our noses and be less alone than we think.

Reading through this reflection, does it resonate with you or with someone you know who is struggling with loneliness? How might you respond in the light of this hope that community may be invisible but right under your nose?

SELINA STONE

Passing on the baton

So Elijah went from there and found Elisha son of Shaphat. He was ploughing with twelve yoke of oxen, and he himself was driving the twelfth pair. Elijah went up to him and threw his cloak around him. Elisha then left his oxen and ran after Elijah. (NIV)

Since Elijah told God that he'd had enough of the prophetic life, God chooses a successor for him so he can retire. Having read Elijah's story, it is perhaps not surprising that he wanted to step back from this work. What might be surprising, however, is how supportive God is of Elijah asserting a boundary and effectively saying 'enough is enough'. God leads Elijah to find Elisha, whom he has called to take over the prophetic work, and Elijah makes it clear that Elisha has a divine assignment to be his apprentice. Elisha drops everything and follows.

We might not be used to thinking about God as someone with whom we can be honest or set a boundary, but truth and boundaries are crucial to authentic and healthy relationships. Pretending that we are okay when we are not is dishonest and carrying on when we have reached our limit – even when it is for a good cause – will surely lead to disaster. So many crises in terms of our own health or that of leaders and communities have occurred because people were not honest with themselves, God or others about their need to step back.

In some cases, a person's identity can be so wrapped up with their role that they refuse to pass it on to anyone else even when it is necessary. Elijah is able to let go of a role which is no longer right for him – he shows us he is willing to serve God and the people of God by handing over the responsibility to Elisha. He models honesty, grace and a healthy relationship to his role, and to the next generation coming behind him – things we can all learn from.

In your own life, is their someone who has passed a baton on to you or someone you are mentoring? If yes, pray for them now, and if not, ask God to provide what you hope for.

SELINA STONE

Life beyond death

As [Jesus] was praying, the appearance of his face changed, and his clothes became as bright as a flash of lightning. Two men, Moses and Elijah, appeared in glorious splendour, talking with Jesus. They spoke about his departure, which he was about to bring to fulfilment at Jerusalem. (NIV)

We do not find any information in the Bible about the end of Elijah's earthly life. He simply fades away in the annals of Israel's history, while the story moves on with his successor Elisha. But that does not mean that his life ends. In the story of the transfiguration, when Jesus goes to pray on a mountain with his close friends, Elijah appears. It isn't clear how the disciples know it is Elijah but the disciples who are with Jesus recognise that it is indeed the old prophet. Elijah somehow pierces the veil of time and eternity to have a conversation with Jesus about his upcoming death.

This episode in Elijah's story lies beyond the usual bounds of time but is important because it highlights the eternal nature of our lives and the ongoing nature of our experience. It can be difficult to imagine our lives after death, and even the most learned theologians will struggle to paint a clear picture. But if this story is anything to go by, it may be that we remain visible and knowable in some mysterious way, and our being after death may not reduce us to mere spirits but will incorporate our bodies.

For Jesus, who is about to cross from this present life to the next, it might have been a comforting moment for him, as he talks with those who have already made the journey. For those of us who have lost loved ones (as I have), Elijah's appearance here might cause us to imagine what it would be like to see them again, and even be able to catch up on all that has been and is to come. For death is not the end.

Lord, thank you that you hold time and eternity in your hands. Though we cannot comprehend death, give us the assurance of your presence even there, and the confidence that you will carry us to the other side. Amen

SELINA STONE

Paying the price

When some of those standing near heard this, they said, 'Listen, he's calling Elijah.' Someone ran, filled a sponge with wine vinegar, put it on a staff, and offered it to Jesus to drink. 'Now leave him alone. Let's see if Elijah comes to take him down,' he said. (NIV)

In this last reflection on Elijah, we find him mentioned as Jesus hangs on the cross at Golgotha. As Jesus cries out the first line of Psalm 22: 'My God, my God, why have you forsaken me', the onlookers think that he is calling out for Elijah. They do not seem to think this is unusual – on the contrary, they consider it to be completely plausible and look to see whether Elijah will appear. We read yesterday that Elijah does appear to Jesus on the mountain of transfiguration, but he does not appear this time and Jesus is left alone.

We know that Elijah is used to the prophetic life in which he stands against political powers, declaring the word of God and being hated for it. He may well identify with Jesus who, in this moment, is paying the ultimate price for disrupting the political and religious powers of his time. Jesus shares the fate of most, if not all, of God's prophets.

As we reflect on the connections between the ministries of Jesus and Elijah, it becomes clear that living a life of faith may involve conflict and tension as much as joy and gentleness. If you are like me, you might prefer to avoid confrontation where possible. But Elijah and Jesus show us that obeying God can require challenging those norms which go against the true love of God and the life and flourishing of God's creation – what we might call sin and death. This might be necessary in our friendships, families, churches, workplaces and online, as we encounter hatred and evil in many forms. In this way, might we take up our crosses and follow the example of Elijah who was believed, even in death, to be a friend of God.

Take some time to reflect on what is happening in the world today. Can you pray about one particular issue and ask God what, if anything, you might do to take a stand, even if it is costly?

SELINA STONE

Images for the Holy Spirit

Fiona Barnard writes:

How do you explain something to those who don't know the vocabulary? In my work as an ESOL tutor (English for speakers of other languages), I often use photos, tell stories or wave my arms around to communicate a word or an idea. Some learners might grasp subtle phrases from the context of a conversation or text. Others, especially beginners, need to see physical objects or images as scaffolding for sentences which will follow. I enjoy creating ways to help the learning process. I love it when understanding dawns and they use words they did not know before.

How can we begin to comprehend who God is and what he has done for us? As we come to celebrate Pentecost, we can be so grateful that the Holy Spirit is the very best tutor, linguist, storyteller and guide. Over the next week, we will ponder some metaphors describing his person and role, pictures which may unpack something of his work.

The Bible offers several images. The Spirit is God's personal presence, active in the world, in the church, in our bodies. He is wind and breath, creating physical and spiritual life. He is associated with fire – consuming, refining and warming hearts. He is gentle as a dove of peace. He is water – drenching, cleansing and refreshing. He is like oil which soothes and heals and separates people for holy purposes. He is an advocate, coming alongside believers and representing them before the Father. He is a counsellor, bringing comfort, clarity and hope. He is a teacher, searching the deep things of God and explaining his word in ways we can understand. He is gift giver and coach, equipping us for service and mission in the world.

In these notes, I have enjoyed employing different metaphors to describe the dynamic person of the Holy Spirit. We explore fresh images to enable us to enter anew the wonder of what he does for us, in us and with us. I pray that the Spirit himself will open our eyes, hearts and minds to all he has given us. May he fill us afresh to tell the story of Jesus and live out the Father's gracious compassion in the world.

'God's love has been poured out into our hearts through the Holy Spirit, who has been given to us' (Romans 5:5, NIV).

Holy dancer

When the Feast of Pentecost came, they were all together... Without warning there was a sound like a strong wind, gale force – no one could tell where it came from... Then, like a wildfire, the Holy Spirit spread through their ranks, and they started speaking in a number of different languages... (MSG)

The Holy Spirit comes dancing into the birth of the church. He swoops into a home in Jerusalem like a mighty rushing wind. He fills the space with his presence and power, with fire and flair. Gusts swirl around the room without blowing out tongues of fire resting gracefully over each head. Caught up in this new, long-awaited movement of God, the disciples are thrust out into the city street, panting, giddy, joyful, overwhelmed by what has happened: God has poured out his Spirit on them! They enter the dance, lifting their eyes towards this new dawn, stretching their minds to grasp the promise fulfilled, gesturing to puzzled observers to join them.

When I try to explain the person and work of the Holy Spirit or the mystery of his relationship with the Father and the Son, it helps to imagine a holy dance. There are times when the Holy Spirit plays a particular role: in creation or new birth, in making us like Jesus or gracing the church with gifts to carry out his mission. Yet the Father and the Son are always on the dance floor, swapping parts, moving and mirroring each other. Together, they weave love and being and action into one.

The Trinity dances and we are invited to be part of this holy music and rhythm. The Spirit teaches us the score and urges us to keep in step with him as the perfect partner. He prays for us when we lose focus and stumble. He picks us up again, saving even our falls as improvisations in his beautiful design. One day, when our bodies are spent, he will carry us to a place where sickness and sorrow and sin are banished. He will transform us in his new creation, where the dance continues.

Today the kingdom dance goes on across the world. As you thank God for the gift of his Spirit, pray for his body, the church, worshipping, interceding, praying, serving and proclaiming good news.

FIONA BARNARD

Holy breath

God formed Man out of dirt from the ground and blew into his nostrils the breath of life. The Man came alive – a living soul! (MSG)

It is a kiss that awakens life. The breath of a handsome prince floods the inert body of Sleeping Beauty. His passion brings vibrant colour to her pale blue lips, vitality to her unmoving limbs. She is loved into life.

Perhaps the universal appeal of this fairytale comes from echoes of earlier stories. At the beginning of time, the dust-formed Adam becomes a living being as the creator God breathes tenderly into his nostrils. Later, an exiled nation, hopeless as a valley of scattered bones, becomes a dynamic Spirit-awakened army in Ezekiel's vision as he calls, 'Come, O breath, from the four winds! Breathe into these dead bodies so they may live again' (Ezekiel 37:9, NLT). Centuries on, an uncertain huddle of believers burst fearlessly on to the street at Pentecost as the Holy Spirit arrives; he appears as gushing wind and fills their lungs and lives with joy, courage and power to speak of Jesus, bringing the church to birth.

When spoken, *Ruach* (pronounced *roo-akh*), the Hebrew word for Spirit, engages the physical act of breathing. It encompasses a range of meanings: of breath that courses through your lungs and body to keep you alive; of wind that cuts you in half, that wrenches an ancient tree from the ground; of breeze that sends autumn leaves into a spin, that refreshes you in the summer heat.

Sometimes it feels as though the world is in meltdown, as crisis after crisis jostles for space in the news headlines: wars, mass migrations, pandemics, environmental catastrophes and economic anxieties. 'There is no God,' cry some. 'Where are you, God?' call others. We cannot see Holy Ruach: dare we trust that he is still present, hovering over the chaos (Genesis 1:2), closer to us than our breath?

Breathe in the love of God: let it go to every cell in your body. Breathe out all that chokes that closeness with him today.

FIONA BARNARD

Holy heart-seeker

Is there any place I can go to avoid your Spirit? to be out of your sight?
If I climb to the sky, you're there! If I go underground, you're there! If I
flew… to the far western horizon, you'd find me in a minute — you're
already there waiting! (MSG)

'She was headhunted for that post,' you hear. 'They wooed her with all manner of enticing promises and perks. Let's hope she can deliver what they
want.' It strikes me that being headhunted could be deemed a compliment,
hampered only by colossal expectations.

As I have considered various ways of describing the Holy Spirit, there is
something about the wooing of a headhunter which chimes: that longing
to bring someone to a new place, a new company, because of their value
and potential. Yet 'hunter' feels like an aggressive word, and 'head' is only
part of what the Spirit desires. So, I have gone for holy heart-seeker, because
the Spirit comes looking for us with the persistence and the grace of a lover,
calling us to enter his embrace with the Father and the Son. That deep
yearning for a closer walk with Jesus, that conscience prick that sends us
to the cross again, that yielding to God's costly will, that salvation joy amid
personal gloom are all evidence of the Spirit seeking us, searching our hearts,
inviting us to know more of him. No human being can manufacture or sell it.
And while the headhunted person may deserve the honour, I know I do not:
the sheer undeserved kindness that God should choose me to be with him,
part of his family, is overwhelming when I let it truly sink in. Grace indeed.

What is more, when I really trust the holy heart-seeker, the pressure
of evangelism is lighter, even if the urgency remains. This week, as I worried about what to say to someone, I noticed one bird following another
effortlessly across the blue sky. 'Holy Spirit,' I prayed, 'please let me follow
you in freedom.' In the conversation that ensued, I was awed by his gentle
presence with us.

---

*Holy heart-seeker, please help me to find the people for whom you are
searching! Amen*

FIONA BARNARD

Holy translator

'He will not speak his own words, but he will speak only what he hears, and he will tell you what is to come. The Spirit of truth will bring glory to me, because he will take what I have to say and tell it to you'. (NCV)

Years ago, as I travelled around Asia, I enjoyed reading notices which had been 'lost in translation'. In the shower: 'Be careful of landslide.' On a train: 'Hang on the safety chair or bar, when door is out of order.' Outside a restaurant called Ireland's Potato: 'Ireland's proverb says there are two things in the world that can't be joked: 1) marriage 2) potato.' While I was grateful for these warnings in English, I realised that electronic decoders may not capture the subtleties of a language. Good translators do not simply spout equivalent words, they weave phrases into meaning and suggest the tone of a sentence. They communicate in ways which elicit understanding and response across linguistic and cultural barriers.

The Holy Spirit is the very best translator. As we seek to comprehend ancient texts written in faraway civilisations, he opens our eyes to their wonder and wisdom. As we follow accounts of wilderness wanderings and prophetic warnings, he points to connections in our own lives. As we read of Jesus, he shows us how we can know our creator through his Son. He is the one who takes the mysterious things of God and translates them into stories and images and truths which turn our lives around.

The holy translator does not work in a vacuum. He uses art and music, experiences and friends, books and study, discussion and sermons. But those moments when the penny drops, when we hear that quiet whisper, when we say, 'Aha, now I see', when we are challenged and moved to love Jesus more: that is the holy translator bringing the glory of Jesus right into our hearts.

I love watching the light go on in a person's eyes when the holy translator is showing them Jesus' truths. Is there someone for whom this is your longing? Pray for them today.

FIONA BARNARD

Holy supporter

God the Father knew you and chose you long ago, and his Spirit has made you holy. As a result, you have obeyed him and have been cleansed by the blood of Jesus Christ. May God give you more and more grace and peace. (NLT)

Have you noticed the subtle shift in our language from the use of the word 'help' to 'support'? Half of me appreciates it, because it feels less patronising. If I see myself as your helper, I may take the ball or the decision out of your hands. If I support you, I encourage your efforts. So, when it comes to the work of the Holy Spirit, what word might we use? He is the one who comes alongside us, as trainer, mentor, encourager. He enables us to play our part in the kingdom of God.

When I am doing a sponsored swim, I ask for support. When I am drowning, I shout, 'Help!' I need the Holy Spirit to do what I cannot do for myself. I cannot rescue myself. I cannot understand the mysteries of God without him revealing them to me. I cannot convert anyone. There are times when I have no love left, situations where I cannot serve with humility and grace. Sometimes I have no words to pray. I need the Holy helper to save me.

Lest I sit back and let the Holy Spirit do everything, he whispers in my ear, 'I am your Holy supporter too. You must commit to continuing on Christ's track even when it is hard. You need to push against the pain barrier. But like a sports coach, I am right by you. The ball is in your court, and so am I. I shape you as you engage in prayer, Bible, meditation and church. We work out together in service to develop spiritual muscle and strength. We note what hinders progress and seek to correct it. We practise together so you are fit to serve God's purposes in the world. We talk so your skills develop not only for spiritual sprints but a lifelong marathon.'

Thank you, Holy Spirit, for working in me to make me holy. Thank you for helping and supporting me as I work out obedience in my daily challenges. Amen
FIONA BARNARD

Holy fruit-grower

The Holy Spirit produces this kind of fruit in our lives: love, joy, peace, patience, kindness, goodness, faithfulness, gentleness and self-control… Since we are living by the Spirit, let us follow the Spirit's leading in every part of our lives. (NLT)

As an earnest teenager, I so wanted to follow Jesus faithfully. In devouring the Bible, I learned what I should be doing and feeling, but struggled to translate it into my everyday living. I read books with stories of the Holy Spirit giving people the power to do wonderful things. I decided a special experience of him could set me up for victory. Perhaps I saw him providing a kind of celestial chocolate which would explode into spiritual energy for the rest of my days. Later, as I wondered what to do with my life, I tried to align the Spirit's gifts described by the apostle Paul with abilities which others claimed to observe in me, though I remained hesitant. Even these spiritual gifts weren't the superfoods that make discipleship and mission healthy and assured.

As I grow older, I realise I am hungry for the wholesome fruit of the Spirit. I long for him to produce in me the character of Jesus. I want to *become* like him rather than *do* marvellous deeds. I am drawn to Christians who keep on keeping on through the decades, faithful in prayer, kind in sharing food, self-controlled in dealing with difficult colleagues, good in choosing justice over convenience, patient in hearing different sides of an argument, gentle in caring for elderly relatives, joyful in their devotion to Jesus.

These delicious fruits take time to develop, from seed to bud to harvest. It is the Spirit who oversees the miracle. He watches and protects. At times, the frost of circumstance may threaten, but the Holy fruit-grower is tending the tree as it weathers rain and wind and sun. He is utterly committed to the crop, to lives of fruitfulness which honour the Son.

Thank you, Holy Spirit, for your commitment to kingdom growth and fruitfulness. I bring you my church today, including those who frustrate me: make us like Jesus as our roots go deep into you. Amen

FIONA BARNARD

Holy *kintsugi*

Be patient with each other, making allowance for each other's faults because of your love. Make every effort to keep yourselves united in the Spirit, binding yourselves together with peace. For there is one body and one Spirit, just as you have been called to one glorious hope for the future. (NLT)

I grew up in a home where everything that could be mended was mended. My mother had regular sessions where broken plates and cups were stuck together with glue. It was not unusual for handles to fall off in the sink again, only to be returned to the repair box. These dishes, even the damaged ones, were too precious to throw away. Each one told a story.

As a Christian, I met that repair box all over again in a church full of broken people with sharp edges and uncertain potential and use. They were not my types. They disturbed my worship of God and my calm service of him: the moody teenager, the managing know-it-all, the manipulative talker, the needy complainer, the leader blind to his faults. 'Lord, get me out of here,' I cried, catapulting my own impatience and judgementalism into the ugly mix.

The Spirit of unity did not let me escape to find more congenial companions. He did something transformational. He showed me that he is the holy glue which binds shattered people into one body, initiated through one baptism into Christ, to honour one Lord, in one faith. The disconnect I felt was nothing in comparison with all I shared with my fellow sinners. The forgiveness I knew in Jesus was more meaningful as it extended to those who had smashed my hopes. The challenge was to bear with their faults as they did with mine. In being 'stuck' with them, the Spirit revealed his deeper ongoing miracle of making us one through nitty-gritty effort and astonishing grace. So, when I heard of *kintsugi*, the ancient Japanese art of fixing broken pottery with lacquers of powdered gold, I knew I had seen that 'golden joinery' in our fragile, precious community of faith.

Spirit of unity, grant me the faith to trace your golden joinery that binds together broken lives and communities when they seem so damaged. May that miracle of healing and peace draw many to you. Amen

FIONA BARNARD

42

What the Bible says about beauty

Lyndall Bywater writes…

Some years ago, I was invited to help make a radio documentary about beauty. The original presenter had moved to the USA to take up a new job and they needed someone to replace her. The concept of the show was a blind person discovering how sighted people perceive beauty, so they needed that someone to be blind. It was a fascinating piece of work to do and I learned a lot, some of which I'll let you in on over the next two weeks.

I remember being amazed by the power of the idea of physical appearance. There are whole industries devoted to helping us change our appearance in the name of beauty, not to mention people who will spend enormous amounts of money trying to change how they look. And lest we roll our eyes in despair, those industries only exist because we humans really are very susceptible to what someone looks like. Appearance, it seems, can get us a job or lose us an election.

One of the interviews I did was with a woman who had recently appeared on the TV show *Love Island*. She talked honestly about how desperate she had been, for most of her life, to change her appearance, and how much money she'd spent on trying to get the look she wanted. As a blind person, the effect was totally lost on me! I couldn't tell whether she looked beautiful or not, but what I could tell very clearly was how beautiful she was on the inside. Her courage, her kindness and her heart for justice shone out. As I listened to her, I found my heart breaking for this woman who had experienced so much pain in the name of physical beauty, while seeming to be so unaware of the beauty within her.

Over the next couple of weeks, we will see what the Bible says about beauty: what real beauty is, where we find it, how God makes it and how we can make it. We'll think a bit about physical appearance, but mostly we'll discover that beauty is a far broader subject than our image-obsessed society might lead us to think.

As we journey together through this most fascinating of topics, my hope and prayer is that you will find beauty in all sorts of places you never imagined you could.

Beautifully good

God saw all that he had made, and it was very good. And there was evening, and there was morning – the sixth day. (NIV)

Have you ever felt damned with faint praise? You know the sort of thing I mean: you've poured your heart and soul into creating something special and you screw up your courage to show it to another human being, only for them to utter the words: 'That's good.' Devastating, isn't it? It conveys a sort of cold indifference. 'Good' is not a word anyone should really be using about things which are breathtakingly wondrous!

That presents us with a bit of a problem when it comes to the creation story. Time and time again, breathtakingly wondrous things spring into life, and God simply says: 'That's good.' If you're a regular reader of the Bible, you'll know that cold indifference is just about the last characteristic we ever see in God, so presumably we need to consider that the word translated here as 'good' might mean something a bit different.

The Hebrew word is *tov*; a tiny word which carries a ton of meaning. It's a word that speaks of something that's wonderful, outstanding, right (as in perfectly fitted to its purpose), joy-bringing and complete. The idea I find most helpful is that *tov* is a sort of 'wow!' God looked at the universe springing into being and said, 'That's… wow!' Where there is *tov*, there is beauty.

There is no evidence anywhere in scripture that God has stopped seeing new life as anything other than *tov*. There has been pride and separation, wrongdoing and pain, but everything God creates is still unfailingly 'wow!' That includes you and me and the world around us. In a world that measures beauty in some fairly unkind ways, know today that, in the eyes of God, you are *tov* – breathtakingly wondrous and unendingly 'wow!' In fact, you're not just *tov*, you're very *tov*.

Creator God, source of all life, all goodness and all beauty, I pause today to thank you for creating me, calling me beautiful and placing me in this glorious world you have made. My heart swells with a 'wow!' of wonder. Amen

LYNDALL BYWATER

Beautiful goodness under construction

'You intended to harm me, but God intended it for good to accomplish what is now being done, the saving of many lives.' (NIV)

Some years ago, one of the London boroughs instigated a knife amnesty. The police set up collection bins where people could deposit their illegal weapons without fear of reprisal. Having collected numerous blades of all types and sizes, an artist was commissioned to make a sculpture out of them. When you consider what some of those knives might have been used for, it truly was the work of bringing beauty out of terrible ugliness.

Yesterday we encountered the word *tov* and delved a little into its meaning, which turns out to be far more complex and exuberant than the word 'good' would imply. Hold that thought as you consider today's passage. Joseph had been treated terribly by his brothers and here they are, at his mercy, a prime target for revenge. Yet that's not what happens next. He doesn't let them off the hook; he confronts them with the reality of the wrong they've done him. But it's as though he can see a glimmer of *tov* at work. From the jagged shards of abuse, abandonment, false accusation and wrongful imprisonment, God has crafted something that's *tov* – not just something that's good, but something that's remarkably beautiful.

We tend to think that things are either beautiful or ugly. If the raw material is beautiful, then the end product will be too. If the raw material is dark, there's no hope of beauty. Yet the Bible portrays beauty as dynamic. God can make beauty even where the raw material is far from good. In fact, the irrepressible creativity of love seems to delight in crafting beautiful goodness out of the things which have caused us most pain in life. Perhaps that's something of what Paul meant when he said that God works all things together for good (Romans 8:28).

Is there part of your story which feels like it can never be anything but ugly? Bring it to God in prayer today, imagining it as a jagged blade which you're handing to God to be sculpted into something beautiful.

LYNDALL BYWATER

Beautiful timing

Yet God has made everything beautiful for its own time. He has planted eternity in the human heart, but even so, people cannot see the whole scope of God's work from beginning to end. (NLT)

Timing really is everything. When I was 12 years old, our school decided to take us into London every Monday to see the sites. We did it all: the Tower of London, St Paul's Cathedral, the Thames Barrier, HMS Belfast, Kew Gardens – quite possibly some of the greatest treasures in the land. But it was all lost on me. I was too young to appreciate any of it. I've visited many of those places since, and the experience has been truly beautiful, but back then it was all just boring.

Yesterday we thought about the story of Joseph and the idea that beauty is dynamic: things that were anything but beautiful can become beautiful in God's hands. This passage from Ecclesiastes continues that thought. Beauty, it seems, has something to do with the right things happening in the right place at the right time. The baking tin removed from the oven half an hour too early may well contain beautiful cake mixture, but it doesn't contain a beautiful cake. The leaves, the buds and even the thorns of a rose bush may well be beautiful, but there are only a few weeks of the year when the full beauty of the rose itself can be seen.

In fact, one translation (the NRSV) of Ecclesiastes 3:11 even swaps the word 'beautiful' for 'suitable', suggesting that beauty is something to do with God bringing things to fullness at exactly the right moment to fulfil their purpose.

When you feel stuck in a season that you're not much enjoying, it's encouraging to know God is making beauty, isn't it? If you wish it was a time to laugh but it just feels like a time to weep, take heart. Seasons turn, and the God who created you can make all things beautiful in their time.

Lord, how well I know the theory but how often I lack the faith. Help me to live wholeheartedly in this present season, whatever it may contain, and teach me to trust that you are indeed making all things beautiful. Amen

LYNDALL BYWATER

Beauty-making

Then Moses said to the Israelites, 'See, the Lord has chosen Bezalel son of Uri, the son of Hur, of the tribe of Judah, and he has filled him with the Spirit of God, with wisdom, with understanding, with knowledge and with all kinds of skills.' (NIV)

I'm just starting a new knitting project. I love knitting, and I also love the challenge of designing my own patterns, but I struggle to make time for it. The idea of creating something beautiful just because I can feels wasteful somehow. Shouldn't I be spending my time on more worthy, more 'productive' things?

If you ever needed to know that God loves arts and crafts, just spend some time in today's passage and in the rest of Exodus 36. The people of Israel have committed to creating a special place to meet with God, and the first thing God tells Moses to do is to find some crafters. Bezalel sounds like a crafter of the highest order: skilled in metalwork, woodwork, textiles, jewellery-making and all kinds of other things. Not only was he skilled, but he was also filled with the Spirit. We think of being Spirit-filled as being about doing church things, but has it ever occurred to you that when you get totally absorbed in creating something, using all your talent to bring forth something beautiful, that it is as Spirit-filled a moment as any great sermon? And beauty isn't just making things that look amazing. Beauty is putting together things that work so that they do what they need to do. Planning, filling in spreadsheets, counting, weighing, measuring, looking after the details – that's all beauty too. How else did the curtains all end up the same size?

It's a wonder to me that God wanted human beings, with all our flaws, to make that most holy of tabernacle tents. God is always about the glorious business of making beauty, and he is always delighted when we join in. Whether we know it or not, whether we believe it or not, we are all capable of making beautiful things.

In what ways do you make beauty? Think beyond arts and crafts. Perhaps you make beauty through your hospitality, your skill at fixing things, your strategising or your love of running. Thank God for that thing today.

LYNDALL BYWATER

Beautiful people with beautiful gifts

And everyone who was willing and whose heart moved them came and brought an offering to the Lord for the work on the tent of meeting, for all its service, and for the sacred garments. (NIV)

I'm part of a community of prayer in Canterbury, and I'll never forget the day we moved into our first building. It was a quirky set of rooms above an estate agent, and we had nothing to put in it, so we'd asked people to bring anything they felt they could donate. We were inundated! Some of it was very useful, while much of it was rather random. But all of it was beautiful to us because it was given in love. We used the talking crocodile cookie jar for years!

Having met Bezalel yesterday, the astonishingly gifted craftsman brought in to lead the tabernacle project, we skip back a chapter today, because to assume it was all down to Bezalel would be a mistake. Before there could be any crafting, sculpting, sewing, gem-setting or carving, there had to be a lot of giving. The Israelites were nomads wandering the wilderness. They couldn't stop off at the local bazaar to buy the materials they needed. The tabernacle had to be built from whatever they already had.

God seems to enjoy it when beauty becomes a joint effort. No one single person could build the tabernacle, not even the immensely talented Bezalel. And no one single gift would have been enough. The finest gold might have been a spectacular contribution, but it wouldn't have been any good for making pillars or curtains. Individuals can produce works of art, but most things of beauty in this world are joint efforts involving many different people and many different gifts.

We humans have a tendency to look for superheroes – individual people who can get the job done single-handedly. In reality, it's when people, with hearts stirred and willing spirits, bring what they have and join together that something truly beautiful can happen.

Think about a community you're a part of, maybe a church, a team or a social group. Give thanks for the contributions different people bring and for the beauty that emerges as a result of those people and those gifts.

LYNDALL BYWATER

Beautiful muscles

Wake up, wake up, O Zion! Clothe yourself with strength. Put on your beautiful clothes, O holy city of Jerusalem… Rise from the dust, O Jerusalem. Sit in a place of honour. Remove the chains of slavery from your neck, O captive daughter of Zion. (NLT)

Our ideas of beauty change from generation to generation and from culture to culture. When I was growing up, the general consensus seemed to be that muscles made a man beautiful but a woman ugly. I like to think things are changing now and that we can see beauty in anyone, no matter their gender or physique.

Today's passage from Isaiah begins with a picture of a woman. Jerusalem and Zion are often addressed in the Old Testament as feminine. This woman is hunched on the floor, bound up in chains, almost comatose in her despair and powerlessness, but it's time for deliverance. The God of love longs to see her free and fully alive. Unlike so many legends and fairy tales, there's no handsome prince come to kiss her awake. God is indeed very much present, ready to bring her comfort and strength, but this is her moment and her choice. She is invited to stand up, to throw off chains (which will involve considerable muscle) and to dress in her own beautiful clothes. This isn't the beauty of well-dressed fragility; this is the beauty of muscle and grit.

Later in the passage, the word 'beautiful' appears again, this time in reference to the feet of a messenger. If you've ever thought about the feet of someone who's run a long way, you'll know they're probably not what we would consider beautiful. Yet to God they are, even with all their grime and callouses.

Sometimes beauty is all about muscle and grit, grime and callouses. When we stand up to fight for freedom, our own and others, it may not always look pretty but it is always beautiful.

Where have you seen beauty in strength recently? Do you know someone who's radiated beauty by taking the hard road, confronting injustice or making some tough choices? Contact them today to tell them of the beauty you see in them.

LYNDALL BYWATER

Beautiful scars

The Lord will hold you in his hand for all to see – a splendid crown in the hand of God. (NLT)

I was brought up to believe that tattoos definitely aren't beautiful. I've never wanted one myself, but I do remember the day I began to change my views. I was reading an article about a woman who had had a tattoo to 'beautify' the scars she bore from years of self-harm. The tattoo didn't hide the scars, it wove around them, and she talked about how life-giving it was to choose to have marks of beauty on her skin to accompany the marks of pain.

Yesterday we reflected on the image of chained, enslaved Jerusalem rising up to claim her freedom. In today's passage, we meet her again and the picture is full of joyful celebration. Yesterday she was a beautiful warrior throwing off oppression. Today she is a crown. In case you're concerned that she's been relegated to fragile prettiness after all that muscle and grit, fear not. This crown is all about strength and authority. Held reverently in the hand of God, this crown draws the eye because this woman has earned respect and honour.

This picture is part of a prophetic prayer, and it's written in the future tense. The writer knows that the nation isn't quite there yet. The trauma of exile and captivity have left their scars, not to mention centuries of making unhealthy choices. But these words are like the tattoo that reminds her that she will one day become all that she is meant to be. The vivid scars and the sparkling gems, they're all part of the beautiful crown which God is so proud to show off to the whole world.

Your scars don't disqualify you; they are simply marks of the journey you've travelled to become the woman you are… a woman of whom God is inordinately proud.

Loving God, help me to love my scars – the physical ones and the emotional ones. Sometimes they're all I can see, but you see so much more in me. Help me to look beyond the scars to see the gems. Amen

LYNDALL BYWATER

Beautiful wisdom

Prize her highly, and she will exalt you; she will honour you if you embrace her. She will place on your head a fair garland; she will bestow on you a beautiful crown. (NRSV)

While undertaking research for the radio documentary on beauty I mentioned in the introduction, I had the opportunity to visit a modelling agency. I asked one of the talent scouts what they look for when recruiting people to join their bank of models. I expected him to outline the gold standard for physical perfection – a symmetrical face, the right kind of eyes, the optimum leg-length and so on – but that wasn't his answer. He took me to the wall where all the models have their pictures displayed and he began to explain what made each face beautiful (in the eyes of the agency at least). In each case, the characteristic he picked out was something distinctive, something unique to that person. It seems individuality is prized in the beauty industry after all!

If the book of Proverbs has a theme, it would be all about finding wisdom. The trouble is, we can end up glorifying wisdom as some kind of mystical gift that only some people can have. I love the fact that this passage equates wisdom with insight, understanding or good sense, depending on which version you read, and those are things any of us can acquire as we make our way through life. For the writer of these verses, wisdom is basically learning as you live; listening to those older and wiser than you; valuing things that matter; discovering how to make good choices. Wisdom is like a friend you get to know better and better, the longer you live.

What that means is that each of us has a different kind of wisdom. The lessons you've learnt are different to the ones I've learnt. No one else has lived your life. The wisdom you've acquired is distinct, unique and beautiful, like a crown designed just for you.

What does your unique wisdom look like? You could try picturing it as a crown, each gem being a lesson you've learnt or a value you hold dear. As you reflect, you might even want to draw or paint it.

LYNDALL BYWATER

The beauty that matters

As a ring of gold in a swine's snout, So is a beautiful woman who is without discretion [her lack of character mocks her beauty]. (AMP)

While presenting the radio documentary on beauty, I got to interview two young women, both in the public eye and both considered above average in beauty. It was fascinating to talk to them about how their looks had opened doors for them and got them opportunities they'd probably never have had otherwise, but it was heartbreaking to hear them talk about the pain of having been rejected out of hand simply because their appearance didn't quite match up to certain standards.

How often do we slip into the trap of thinking life would be better if we looked more beautiful? This passage is about how wisdom, kindness, generosity and integrity are the qualities that matter most. The idea of a gold ring in a pig's snout may sound rather cute to us, but to a readership who believed pigs to be unclean, it would have been a shocking statement. The writer was effectively saying that it would be obscene to be physically beautiful without having a character to match.

And yet, as my two interviewees can attest, we still live in a world that puts far too much value on physical appearance. I am blind, so their looks were lost on me, but I found myself marvelling at the strength and beauty of each woman's character shining through, and I found myself wondering how we can do more to champion the importance of inner beauty above physical appearance. Could we perhaps make sure that every time we compliment someone on their appearance, we also compliment them on an aspect of their character that we admire? Or, next time we see someone in the media who's beautiful, could we find out a bit more about them and pray for them?

Lord, forgive us for the ways in which our society still puts too much emphasis on physical appearance. Teach us to do the harder work of getting to know people properly, so we can discover the beauty of their inner selves. Amen
LYNDALL BYWATER

To beautify or not to beautify

What matters is not your outer appearance – the styling of your hair, the jewellery you wear, the cut of your clothes – but your inner disposition. Cultivate inner beauty, the gentle, gracious kind that God delights in. (MSG)

I grew up in The Salvation Army, and one of my earliest memories of going to church was the rule that we weren't allowed to wear any jewellery with our junior soldier's uniform. Not wearing jewellery with a uniform isn't unusual, but to me as a child it simply communicated the message that I shouldn't try to look pretty or in any way distinctive when I came to worship.

The debate about whether women should or shouldn't dress to look beautiful has raged on for centuries, and today's passage has been right in the thick of it. Some parts of the church revel in the beauty of lavish clothes and adornments, believing that fine things bring God glory. Others, like the part of the church I grew up in, fear that opulence distracts us from God. The sad result is that women (and it usually has been women) have been left feeling guilty, either for wanting to dress to look beautiful or for not having the means to dress smartly enough.

I think we would all agree that what's on the inside is far more important than a person's outward appearance, but I am struck today by the end of verse 6, which *The Message* version renders as 'unanxious and unintimidated'. That sounds gloriously liberating to me. What if we didn't feel anxious about our outward appearance, knowing that God loves us as we are. What if we didn't feel intimidated by the opinions of others, knowing that when we use our clothing, make-up and jewellery to express our personalities, the world is a richer place.

Personal appearance is a personal matter, but this passage also challenges us to relate to each other in mutual love and respect, and that's something beautiful which this often divided, polarised world really needs.

Lord, save us from our centuries-old sin of tearing each other apart over the way we dress. Stir us to mutual love and respect, helping one another to shake off anxiety and intimidation about the way we look. Amen

LYNDALL BYWATER

Nourishing beauty

Finally, brothers and sisters, whatever is true, whatever is noble, whatever is right, whatever is pure, whatever is lovely, whatever is admirable – if anything is excellent or praiseworthy – think about such things.' (NIV)

What do you do to refresh yourself? Do you love to read a good book, go for a walk in nature, listen to music, enjoy a TV programme or indulge in a spectacularly good coffee? Maybe your perfect day off includes all of the above.

Has it ever occurred to you that the vast majority of the things we do for relaxation and fun have something to do with beauty? An author has taken time to craft the plot and the prose of the book you're enjoying; musicians have used their skills to produce the music you love; a whole string of people deployed their talents to produce your favourite cup of coffee and, of course, the walk in nature allows you to feast your eyes on the beauty of creation.

We have talked a lot about our own beauty over the past few days, but beauty is something we encounter in all sorts of ways and is vital to the well-being of our souls. Perhaps that's why Paul tells us to fix our minds on things which are beautiful (that's my shorthand for his comprehensive list of adjectives). When anxiety wears us down, when peace is hard to find, when joy seems to be unreachable, we search out beauty, and somehow it connects us to heaven.

I love that remarkable scene in the film *The Shawshank Redemption* where one of the prisoners plays an opera aria through the prison's tannoy system, and the inmates are transported for just a few moments to a different reality. That's what beauty does for us.

We understand the importance of a healthy diet, a regular exercise routine and even things to keep our minds agile, but do we pay attention to our need for beauty?

What are the beautiful things which you enjoy so much that they can really occupy your mind and draw your attention away from your cares and worries? How can you build those things into the rhythms and routines of your life?

LYNDALL BYWATER

Exquisite beauty

Then Mary took about half a litre of pure nard, an expensive perfume; she poured it on Jesus' feet and wiped his feet with her hair. And the house was filled with the fragrance of the perfume. (NIV)

A woman knew she was going to spend time with Jesus. This man had shown her the way back to life and hope. For all she knew, he might have been God. He certainly felt like God to her. Beautiful times call for beautiful gifts, and so she brought the most beautiful thing she owned.

Thanks to the stingy attitude of the dinner guests in today's story, our attention is immediately drawn to how much the bottle of nard cost and what a sacrificial offering it was for her to make, but that totally misses the point. Yes, nard was expensive, but first and foremost it was beautiful. Its exquisite fragrance would have filled the house, stopped people in their tracks, hung in the air for weeks. It would have clung to Jesus' skin, hair and clothes for days. He would still have been smelling it as they nailed him to a cross several days later. The woman brought intoxicating beauty to that dinner party, and promptly used it all on Jesus in one of the most sacred moments of his earthly life. And he welcomed it, not pushing her away but revelling in it.

Johannes Hartl, leader of the Augsburg House of Prayer, once gave a talk that brought my praying to life in a new way. It was all about how spending time in God's presence is the most beautiful thing we can ever do. We should therefore do it with a joyous abandon, not trying to make our prayer times as efficient and productive as possible, but making them sumptuously lavish, filling them with beautiful art and music, breathtaking nature, even delicious food, because to spend time with God is to be in the most beautiful company in the universe, and that deserves to be celebrated.

How might you bring beauty to your prayer times? Is there a piece of art or music you love which you could bring to God? Give yourself permission to enjoy revelling in something beautiful next time you pray.

LYNDALL BYWATER

Beautiful provision

'And why worry about your clothing? Look at the lilies of the field and how they grow. They don't work or make their clothing, yet Solomon in all his glory was not dressed as beautifully as they are.' (NLT)

During the Covid-19 lockdowns, those who had to shield at home began to receive food parcels from the Government. We quickly realised that those parcels were adequate but very basic, and so some churches and charities worked together to supplement them with fresh food. People were amazed and astonished to find such beautiful food arriving on their doorsteps when all they'd expected was a pack of the basics.

Today's passage may be rather familiar to you, but have you ever noticed the role beauty plays in it? We think of it as a reassuring promise from Jesus that all of our needs will be met, and it certainly is that, but it contains something more. It contains not only a promise to provide for us but also a promise to lavish beauty on us. I imagine Jesus sitting in front of a huge crowd of people, pointing to birds flying overhead or flowers growing nearby. He doesn't say: 'Your Father in heaven keeps those birds and flowers alive, so he'll keep you alive too.' He says something to the effect of: 'Those birds and flowers have beauty that even the wealthiest, most powerful king you can think of didn't have. So while your Father in heaven is keeping you alive, he'll also be decking you out in beauty.'

The past few years have been tough on many of us, and it may well be that you've struggled to make ends meet. Divine provision rarely makes us rich, but it does tend to come with a side order of beauty; whether that's a deeper trust in God learnt through the hard times or deeper relationships with family, friends and neighbours as we learn to support each other. God always wants to give us more than just the basics.

Could you be part of the gift God is giving someone else? Is there someone whose immediate need you know you can't meet, but who you could still bless with something beautiful? Remember, beauty doesn't have to cost a penny.

LYNDALL BYWATER

Beauty himself

The servant grew up before God – a scrawny seedling, a scrubby plant in a parched field. There was nothing attractive about him, nothing to cause us to take a second look. He was looked down on and passed over, a man who suffered, who knew pain firsthand. One look at him and people turned away. (MSG)

One of the things I learnt while researching for the radio documentary is just how much of a role beauty plays in people's voting. We are apparently much more likely to consider voting for someone if we like how they look, regardless of what their policies or values may be. We make swift judgements about people just from glimpsing a face for a fraction of a second, and that first impression is very hard to change once it's been made.

We close our series of reflections on beauty today by thinking about the most beautiful human being there has ever been. Artists down the centuries have sought to capture how he looked, but I'm not sure most of them have really taken this verse from Isaiah seriously. Jesus is so often portrayed as someone who looks beautiful, whether it's the blonde-haired, blue-eyed version or the more authentic Middle Eastern one. Yet this prophecy suggests that Jesus wasn't beautiful – not outwardly, anyway. There was nothing about his physical appearance that would have drawn us to him (or made us want to vote for him). If the research on beauty is to be believed, the vast majority of people would have taken one look at him and written him off. And that makes it all the more remarkable that he was inundated with people who wanted to be near him.

I suspect it was no coincidence that children loved to be near Jesus. They have a knack for not being put off by outward appearance, and they often have an instinct for who is good, real and safe. Those who became his followers were those who could see beauty of the non-physical variety; people who could tune into the beauty of a life lived and laid down in love.

Jesus, forgive me when I'm distracted by outward appearances. Open the eyes of my heart to see beauty wherever it resides. Teach me to fix my gaze on you, the source of all that is truly beautiful in this life. Amen

LYNDALL BYWATER

Jesus, the healer

Lakshmi Jeffreys writes:

The Green Mile is a favourite film of the Most Revd Justin Welby (archbishop of Canterbury from 2013). It is powerful and disturbing but ultimately a hope-filled story of prisoners and guards on death row in 1930s Louisiana. The central prisoner, John Coffey, is a huge, illiterate African American, who has remarkable healing abilities. As the story progresses, fascination grows with this man and his interactions with others. John Coffey is not meant to be Jesus and the plot is not an allegory of the gospel, but the parallels with aspects of Jesus' life are striking and indicate how people beyond the church are fascinated by healing and especially by the person with healing powers. The range of hospital and other dramas involving doctors, nurses or similar roles on film and television, to say nothing of literature and art throughout history, indicate human interest. Coming from a family of doctors (while lacking formal medical training beyond a Brownie's first aid badge), I share a near obsession with such matters!

In Luke's gospel there are more than 20 examples of Jesus healing different people. (It is worth reading or listening to this gospel in one or two sittings to experience how frequently healing is mentioned.) This is hardly surprising given that Luke is described as a physician and would have a natural inclination towards this aspect of Jesus' ministry. The key, though, is not the healing events themselves, however dramatic. Instead, the focus is the context. What is Jesus saying about God's kingdom, about how people behave and about who God is? Hence, this series concentrates on Jesus at the centre of each episode, rather than what happened.

Your church might offer healing services. You or someone you know might have experienced God's healing. On the other hand, you might find it hard to accept that supernatural healing takes place today. After all, the miracles of technology and science allow people to recover from conditions which not long ago might have ended their lives. Whatever your views, I invite you, over the next couple of weeks, to explore familiar stories through the lens of Jesus the healer and perhaps discover your place in God's unfolding story.

God on God's terms

'The Spirit of the Lord is upon me, because he has anointed me to bring good news to the poor. He has sent me to proclaim release to the captives and recovery of sight to the blind, to let the oppressed go free, to proclaim the year of the Lord's favour.' (NRSV)

Jesus set out his manifesto, in fact his purpose, in a synagogue in his hometown of Nazareth. After his reading from Isaiah, the congregation were electrified. Doubtless they thought they were in for a treat – after all, there were reports of what Jesus had achieved elsewhere and here he was reading about miraculous healing. Imagine their dismay when Jesus not only stated he would not perform for them, but also reminded the people that God worked on God's terms and often for 'outsiders' rather than those who considered themselves special to God.

Jesus the healer is God in human form. Of course, we know this, but sometimes we focus either on the supernatural God-aspect of Jesus or on the man who calls us friend and who understands emotions, temptations and other facets of being a person. Both extremes lead us to disappointment or worse. As C.S. Lewis described in the Narnia books: 'Aslan is not a tame lion.' In other words, Jesus can and does heal, but we do not own Jesus. He invites us to pray, honestly and openly from the heart, but we are not to determine the outcome. Perhaps this is because our vision is so much smaller than God's. Jesus came to set the world free from sin, sickness and all that is wrong. Salvation of the world God so loves is not limited to God's people or to those individuals and circumstances we feel deserve healing. This can challenge our prayers for healing and restoration.

At the time of writing, there are certain international and personal conflicts where right and wrong seem obvious to me. Perhaps I need to focus on God as God is and then hold before God those for whom I ache.

Slowly read through today's verses, recognising God is creator, Son and Holy Spirit. Then notice how and with whom God performed miracles. Now pray for yourself and the people and situations on your heart.

LAKSHMI JEFFREYS

Authority and response

Amazed, the people exclaimed, 'What authority and power this man's words possess! Even evil spirits obey him, and they flee at his command!' (NLT)

Power is the ability to do something, while authority is the right to do something. I have learned as much about authority from having a dog as from being a mother! Unlike a baby, the dog is not learning to speak as she hears my voice. She reacts to who and how I am, more than the actual words I use, although she recognises several such as 'sit', 'come', 'wait' and various people's names. Of course, the tone of my voice is important, but it takes more than a loud, clear command for the dog to do what is required. She responds better when I speak with authority, rather than simply power.

Jesus read the words in the synagogue as countless others had before, but he was different. Somehow the words meant something. Jesus was both proclaiming the coming of the promised kingdom of God and living it. As a result, evil spirits and diseases left the sufferers and, as we see with Peter's mother-in-law, the person who had been healed responded to Jesus' authority by attending him. I wonder if this nameless woman was included in the biblical text as an example of someone who served after receiving God's blessing.

Often, we pray for someone to be set free from physical pain or suffering – and this is good and right. But there are occasions when someone responds to Jesus' authority and not only grows in faith themselves, but also brings others to faith – without experiencing physical healing and sometimes even dying. Once again, the only way to make sense of the situation is to focus on Jesus and to cry out with our questions, while continuing, if so led, to pray for miraculous physical restoration. Jesus has authority to heal in every way. Lord, I believe; help my unbelief…

Loving God, I don't understand why some people are freed from diseases and evil spirits and others are not. Teach me to trust you, to recognise your healing and respond to your call to serve in your kingdom. Amen

LAKSHMI JEFFREYS

Authority questioned

Jesus said to the man, 'Young man, your sins are forgiven.' But the Pharisees and teachers of religious law said to themselves, 'Who does he think he is? That's blasphemy! Only God can forgive sins!' (NLT)

Joanne (not her real name) has given permission for this story to be shared.

Joanne and her husband, Jonathan, were members of their local church. Jonathan had requested prayer for healing from unbearable headaches but there had been little relief. Gradually Jonathan stopped going to church. Some weeks later, Jonathan left Joanne for the woman with whom he had been conducting an adulterous affair for several months. His headaches were related to his behaviour, at odds with his relationship with God.

Increasingly, the western world is catching up with the global south in recognising the link between physical, mental, emotional and spiritual well-being. Jesus' manifesto was to release people from oppression and proclaim the coming of the time of the Lord's favour. But before we can receive the Lord's favour, God needs to rid us of all that gets in the way of open relationship.

The Pharisees were correct in their assertion that only God could forgive sins. They simply could not cope with Jesus' undoubted authority, proved when the paralysed man was able to walk at Jesus' command. This challenged their reliance on outward appearance and status, rather than obedience to God. And yet the passage begins with a statement about how the religious leaders were following Jesus from place to place. As with Jonathan, there was both fascination with and a desire to encounter Jesus – but on their own terms.

God speaks in many ways. How often we miss 'body wisdom' – physical signals which can be symptoms of deeper malaise, as with Jonathan. When I have certain pain in my shoulders, I have learned I am bearing emotional burdens that do not belong to me. As I come before Jesus, he shows me the root of the problem and the next step to manage it.

Pray that you might grow in both 'body wisdom' and courage, to come before Jesus – and bring others to him – not as spectators but to submit to his authority.

LAKSHMI JEFFREYS

Do good

Jesus said to [the religious leaders], 'I ask you, is it lawful to do good or to do harm on the sabbath, to save life or to destroy it?' After looking around at all of them, he said to [the man with the withered hand], 'Stretch out your hand.' (NRSV)

Rules and lists help me to feel safe. Until the Covid-19 lockdowns, I used to make a two-month list of all our evening meals. At the beginning of each month, I filled the freezer and cupboard with whatever could be stored, buying perishables as they were needed. I rarely stuck to the menu; instead, every meal was 'elastic' – able to stretch to feed whoever was at the table. If we were eating elsewhere, the meal of the day was enjoyed on another occasion. The list (now monthly) ensured there were sufficient ingredients to make wholesome food every day.

Continuing with this monthly menu as an analogy, the scribes and Pharisees who were angry with Jesus might have been cross if we had consumed pasta on Monday instead of the stated rice. But they would have missed the purpose of the list and the needs of the people around the table. These leaders were livid when Jesus healed on the sabbath, regardless of the opportunity to bring life and freedom. In verse 31, Jesus summarises the blessings and woes: 'Do to others as you would have them do to you.' This statement offers the purpose of the law, regardless of whether it is the sabbath: love others (whoever they are) as we love ourselves.

Jesus was always aware of the purpose – of healing, of the sabbath, of religious law. He was conscious of the people around him and, above all, of God's call on his life. Love of God, others and self, defines faith beyond religious observance. God's law makes sense only when we live in the light of God's love – demonstrated through prayerful, selfless and loving actions.

Free me, gracious God, from adherence to rules or duty alone. Teach me to do good: to see as you see and thereby to act justly, love mercy and walk humbly with you (Micah 6:8). Amen

LAKSHMI JEFFREYS

Good news for all?

[Jesus] said, 'I tell you, not even in Israel have I found such faith'…
[The people] glorified God, saying, 'A great prophet has risen among
us!' and 'God has looked favourably on his people!' (NRSV)

In many examples of healing in Luke's gospel, Jesus responds to the suf-
ferer. Today's stories are slightly different. In the first, it is not the centurion
himself who asks for his slave to be healed but the local leaders, who love
this Roman soldier, despite his being a Gentile and an enemy. In the second, Jesus is moved with compassion when he sees the widow whose son
has died. Jesus' amazement at the centurion's faith is matched by that of
the crowd in Nain, who witness a dead young man being restored to life.
In both cases – indeed, on every occasion Jesus heals – the good news of
God's salvation can be seen and experienced. When God's kingdom is fully
established, there will be no more sin, sickness or death. Meanwhile, Jesus'
actions offer glimpses of how life will be then.

It is easy to focus on direct physical healing and how much better life
will be (for the centurion, his servant, the widow, etc.). This is natural and
important. But equally significant is the wider context – additional signs
of God's kingdom and Jesus being recognised for who he is, the author
of healing and the source of everlasting good news. We lose sight of the
latter at our peril.

One member of a local family, none of whom is yet involved in church,
has a debilitating physical condition. They have occasionally allowed me –
and once or twice other Christians from our church – to pray for them. Our
daily prayer is for God to heal this person physically and to restore the
family to life. We are also praying that they will recognise the God who has
healed them all. Writing these notes shows me that I have not yet sought
a kingdom perspective: Jesus' good news may be something other than
immediate physical healing.

---

*How do you pray for healing? How does Jesus want you to pray? How does
he want to show you the kingdom and, perhaps, even heal you?*

LAKSHMI JEFFREYS

News of good news

'Go and tell John what you have seen and heard: the blind receive their sight, the lame walk, the lepers are cleansed, the deaf hear, the dead are raised, the poor have good news brought to them. And blessed is anyone who takes no offence at me.' (NRSV)

Life had never been easy for John the Baptist. The only child of much older parents, he had a strange diet, unique taste in clothes and lived in a less than desirable area. He knew of his cousin Jesus and was well versed in the signs of God's coming kingdom. Following an altercation with King Herod Antipas, John was now in prison. The Messiah was supposed to come like Elijah, bringing down fire from heaven, but nothing of the sort had been reported. Instead, Jesus was an itinerant preacher, loved by crowds and hated by the religious authorities – similar but different to John. Had John got everything wrong?

John's ministry was primarily to bring people to repentance. Jesus' task was to bring life and wholeness – shalom, complete well-being. After reminding John of all the healing taking place, Jesus seemed to say that someone would be blessed if they took Jesus for who he was, without preconceived ideas! Jesus' response to John offered different signs of the kingdom and aspects of the Messiah. As a result, the good news was not what John had expected.

The ability to recognise God's good news goes beyond finding a silver lining in a passing (or apparently permanent) cloud or 'spinning' a story. Society is bombarded by bad news – items packaged so that we feel scared or sad or angry. As a result, some people share bad news more readily than good and this can be draining. Perhaps Christians can develop the ability to know God so well that we recognise God's work and can celebrate this, however small. At the beginning of the invasion of Ukraine by Russia in 2022, Christian churches worked and prayed together in creative ways. This, as well as the practical outcome for refugees and others, was worth celebrating.

How might you discover and share God's good news, beyond spin or 'looking on the bright side', in every conversation you have today? It could require prayerful discipline!

LAKSHMI JEFFREYS

Jesus and women

[Jesus was accompanied by his disciples and] some women who had been cured of evil spirits and diseases. Among them were Mary Magdalene, from whom he had cast out seven demons; Joanna, the wife of Chuza, Herod's business manager; Susanna; and many others who were contributing from their own resources. (NLT)

'Hello. It's only me…' Do you know women who begin phone conversations in this manner? The 'only' sounds as if the speaker is apologising for herself. Should she be bothering you, since you are so busy, too important to be troubled by her? On the other hand, you might be someone who considers yourself 'only _' (insert your name). This is a real shame. The Bible says you were knit together in your mother's womb – fearfully and wonderfully made – in the image of God. Moreover, Jesus calls you by name and accepts you – as he called and accepted the women in today's reading.

The inclusion of the women, some by name, is extraordinary. In Jesus' day, Jewish women and men did not associate in public. For a rabbi to have female disciples and for them to travel with him was almost unheard of. Moreover, some of these women appeared to be financially independent (or to have generous, trusting husbands) and were thereby able to support Jesus and the other disciples. It is impossible to know how many women, in addition to Joanna, were married. If they were, they must have left their families, albeit temporarily, to follow Jesus.

We are also not told how many of the unnumbered women had been healed. In the society of Jesus' day, women had little social status, despite the family matriarch having considerable power. But a woman who had certain diseases would have been considered unclean and one who appeared to have an evil spirit or was possessed by demons would have been shunned.

Jesus now, as then, does not label women as society might. He accepts us as we are, healing us of anything that would hinder our discipleship. You and I are never 'only' anyone!

Gracious God, thank you for calling me to be a disciple of Christ. Forgive me for denigrating myself in any way. Help me to believe you have chosen me and you love me. Teach me to act and speak from this truth. Amen

LAKSHMI JEFFREYS

Public and private (1)

There came a man named Jairus, a leader of the synagogue. He fell at Jesus' feet and begged him to come to his house, for he had an only daughter, about twelve years old, who was dying. (NRSV)

Given the opposition to Jesus by various religious leaders, Jairus must have been desperate – and who can blame him. Although death can be a release from pain, indignity or unbearable suffering, it always seems wrong for a parent to outlive their child. God weeps with those who weep, particularly when people are bereft of the younger generation. As a mother, I have witnessed first-hand how rapidly a child's health can deteriorate – and, thankfully, be restored. It must have been excruciating as Jesus initially battled slowly through the crowds before stopping. I can only begin to imagine the extent of Jairus' numbness and swirling emotions when greeted with the news that his daughter had died.

Who informed the rest of the world of the events in the dead girl's room, when Jesus entered with five significant adults? After all, Jesus had made it clear that no one should tell what happened. There is a sharp contrast between the public declaration of Jairus' request and the almost secret nature of the healing. As usual, Jesus is dealing with the people in front of him. It is only proper that personal family matters remain private. Even if Jairus was considered public property, his wife and daughter were not.

The world at large has always been fascinated by the private lives of people in the public eye, whether politicians, actors, teachers or even church leaders. Unwise use of social media or press intrusion can blur the distinction between job and home, sometimes leading to heartache. The Bible has harsh words about gossip, and Jesus respects the person beyond the role. We would do well to remember this.

Pray for people you know who have a public-facing role, however large or small – and pray especially for their families and friends.

LAKSHMI JEFFREYS

Public and private (2)

She declared in the presence of all the people why she had touched him, and how she had been immediately healed. He said to her, 'Daughter, your faith has made you well; go in peace.' (NRSV)

The healing of the woman with the haemorrhages for twelve years (yes, the same as the age of Jairus' daughter) is nestled between the passages we explored yesterday. Any of us who has struggled with heavy periods or other menstruation complexities might understand the woman's shame and fear. In addition, her condition rendered her unclean. No one could touch her since direct physical contact caused them to be contaminated. I don't know how you coped during the coronavirus pandemic, but many women I speak to struggled with isolation. Imagine being physically, emotionally and socially isolated for more than a decade!

For any or all the stated reasons, the woman wanted to access Jesus' healing power unnoticed. Like Jairus, she must have been desperate. If she were discovered, she risked total humiliation, to say nothing of potentially tainting a famous rabbi. Yet her courageous action was spectacularly rewarded. Notice how Jesus addresses her. The unnamed outcast is acknowledged before the crowd as 'daughter', a faith-filled member of God's family.

Jesus respected people but exposed sin, evil and, here, disease. So often, we fear naming an illness because that makes it real. But, when we trust Jesus, we can be honest with him and with ourselves. A Christian friend had a colleague who was terrified of an impending mammogram. My friend quietly prayed for the woman before and during the examination, and again as the results were shared. Facing her fear with a Christian, the woman was able to experience something of God's peace.

Perhaps we can help society overcome the fear and embarrassment sometimes associated with menopause, periods, breast issues and other gynaecological matters, as we share them with God and one another.

Pray for women who live in fear and embarrassment because of a health matter. Pray for medical and other personnel who seek to help.

LAKSHMI JEFFREYS

Healing, kingdom and discipleship

[Jesus] gave them power and authority over all demons and to cure diseases, and he sent them out to proclaim the kingdom of God and to heal. (NRSV)

Here Jesus offers his disciples 'see one, do one, teach one' training. These stories show the disciples healing people (or not) and are interspersed with words and miracles indicating the nature of God's kingdom and the centrality of the cross. The overall purpose was to bring God's peace, shalom, to individuals and communities. Sometimes this was successful, but occasionally Jesus had to step in. While Jesus had given the disciples both power and authority, it seems they had learned by rote, without really understanding the task.

Curing diseases, casting out demons, proclamation of the kingdom of God and healing are distinct but linked. Central to each is faith in Jesus and willingness to follow the way of the cross. It is not surprising that the disciples failed to grasp what Jesus said about his eventual betrayal, suffering and death. When someone is making a radical, positive, life-giving difference, the last thing anyone wants to hear is that they will be going away – in a deeply unpleasant manner. If that was the excuse for the disciples' lack of faith and effectiveness, what is ours?

One of my current concerns is 'functional atheism'. This is when we do and say 'the right thing' without really engaging with God. I have yet to meet anyone who, at some point, has not simply gone through the motions. Healing, kingdom and discipleship arise when Jesus is the focus: all our words and actions emanate from him. Using these notes is a start and you might try silent prayer, not asking God for anything but listening. Other disciplines include regular sabbath (days to rest with God), fasting, acts of service, time with someone you trust who will ask challenging questions about where your focus really is – the list is endless.

Is God inviting you to see, do or teach in order to experience God's shalom and to share it with others? If you are unsure, try one of the spiritual disciplines mentioned and see what happens after a month.

LAKSHMI JEFFREYS

Who is in charge?

'Whoever is not with me is against me, and whoever does not gather with me scatters'. (NRSV)

When someone other than the disciples was casting out demons, Jesus commented that whoever was not against them was for them (Luke 9:50). He now appears to say completely the opposite! The difference is the context. On this occasion, some people are suspicious about the authority and source of Jesus' healing power. Clearly Jesus can perform supernatural feats – but so can the devil. Whose side is Jesus really on? To address these matters, and when berated again for healing on the sabbath, Jesus reminds everyone present about God's kingdom.

God's kingdom is where and when people live by God's rules on God's terms. Signs of God's kingdom include life, healing, love and all the fruit of the Holy Spirit. Anything which promoted these aspects of life, Jesus said, was not far from the kingdom. In God's kingdom, the rule of love trumps other regulations. Even the people in the synagogue knew this and were ashamed of treating their animals better than they were allowing Jesus to treat the elderly woman he healed.

Do you remember WWJD ('What would Jesus do?') bracelets? They were a brilliant idea, but the wearer was not Jesus. Jesus observed God's law as God intended. When he healed on the sabbath, Jesus was not working to earn money or better himself – he was demonstrating love. A more accurate bracelet would have the initial letters for 'What did Jesus do and how was he adhering to God's law, even when he appeared to be breaking the rules?' (Perhaps that is more of a necklace!)

God's kingdom comes when God is central. As I pray and focus on the other person, I no longer work for praise or approval and the glory goes to God.

If you are uncertain about your motives for something but genuinely want God to be in charge, pray and then get on with it. You can repent later if necessary!
LAKSHMI JEFFREYS

Faith, duty and thankfulness

'The servant does not deserve thanks for obeying orders, does he? It is the same with you; when you have done all you have been told to do, say, "We are ordinary servants; we have only done our duty."' (GNT)

I love the story of Jesus healing ten people with skin diseases. They chose to be outcasts together. They realised Jesus had the power and authority to transform them. The person who came back to Jesus was thought to be an enemy of God's people. Doubtless the others were also grateful to be restored to health and to their community, but perhaps they took for granted who Jesus was and what he did. The one who returned saw beyond his own needs, to express thankfulness to the one who changed his life. He is an example of an outsider being more alert to the things of God.

Faith, duty and thankfulness are associated because none of these attitudes takes God for granted. When people say, 'I wish I had your faith', they betray a lack of understanding that faith is trust in the person and work of Jesus Christ, rather than desperately but vaguely hoping. In our society, duty is considered an outdated concept – life is more about feelings and desires. We forget that although we are beloved children of God, we are still under his authority. While God owes us nothing, we owe God everything in response to Jesus' life, death and resurrection.

Someone in the local pub once asked me about Lent. She loved the idea of both giving up something and creating a good habit. In her case, this was a 'gratitude journal'. Every time I see her, she tells me how the journal enhances her life and how she failed to maintain the fasting habit. An 'attitude of gratitude' is important for good mental health, but thankfulness, linked with faith and duty, transforms relationships, as we recognise ourselves in God's sight and express this in every aspect of life.

Heavenly Father, thank you for your amazing love. Teach me to respond to you with thankful service. Amen

LAKSHMI JEFFREYS

What do you want me to do for you?

He cried out, 'Jesus! Son of David! Have mercy on me!'... Jesus stopped and ordered the blind man to be brought to him. When he came near, Jesus asked him, 'What do you want me to do for you?' 'Sir,' he answered, 'I want to see again.' (GNT)

The teenager with an eating disorder wanted her mother to make it go away, so that she would not feel fat. The woman with an abusive former partner wanted him to change, so that she could reconnect with mutual friends. I want the builders to complete repairs to the church so that I don't have to think about what to transport to other locations for services. None of these desires answers the question Jesus asked the blind man: 'What do you want me to do for you?' In each case, the individual wants transformation without personal engagement or recognition of who Jesus is. For example, I simply want the building problem to go away and would love Jesus to 'sort it', rather than coming before Jesus and discovering his desires for me.

The blind man, on the other hand, immediately realised Jesus' significance. While the crowd recognised Jesus from Nazareth, who did amazing things, the blind man gave him the title 'Son of David'. Here was the promised Messiah. (The blind man seemed to realise what John the Baptist did not – see earlier notes.) Indeed, the blind man not only knew who Jesus was but also grasped the requirement to first ask for mercy, rather than demand a particular outcome. Of course, his need was obvious, but Jesus allowed him the dignity of a personal request. Once this was granted, everyone praised and glorified God. This was not simply about a blind man getting what he wanted: instead, here was the king at work, in the middle of his kingdom. It is no coincidence that this took place as Jesus was approaching Jerusalem for his crucifixion.

What do you want Jesus to do for you? Come before the Holy One and ask.

LAKSHMI JEFFREYS

Deliver us from evil

He touched the man's ear and healed him. Then Jesus said… 'I was with you in the Temple every day, and you did not try to arrest me. But this is your hour to act, when the power of darkness rules.' (GNT)

It was tempting to end this series of notes considering Jesus' healing words on the cross to the thief who acknowledged him or to the travellers on the road to Emmaus. Instead, I have chosen to concentrate on the final act of physical healing by Jesus in Luke's gospel. From the time Jesus prays in the garden of Gethsemane to his resurrection appearances, he is most obviously the central character. His anguish at the suffering he must endure, alongside the sadness of betrayal and the apparent triumph of evil, do not stop him from serving his enemies – not only the soldiers and religious leaders but now, it seems, also his disciples. He prevents fighting and possibly further arrests and restores the soldier's ear before facing the final task to fulfil his purpose.

These studies on Jesus the healer have offered vignettes of healing miracles, their author and how we might respond. We have learned that we demonstrate Christian discipleship when we submit to Jesus, rather than simply observe and attempt to copy what he said and did. This requires us to come daily before God to rediscover who God is and who we are in his service. We need to repent, rejoice, cry out, be thankful and otherwise be honest about what we want Jesus to do for us and for those around us.

Whatever your views on healing miracles, Jesus has chosen you and me to work with God to demonstrate God's kingdom rule. This includes sharing good news in word and deed, healing relationships and emotions and, if called, offering prayer-fuelled physical restoration. We make personal sacrifices as we serve God and our neighbours. As we pray for the Holy Spirit to work in and through us, we too shall experience healing and transformation, overcome evil and give glory to God.

If you are able, make time to dwell with the final three chapters of Luke's gospel and discover how Jesus remains the healer, bringing in God's kingdom, through and beyond death. Note your response.

LAKSHMI JEFFREYS

Judges: not how things should be

Sara Batts-Neale writes:

A few years ago, a non-church friend was amazed to find Samson and Delilah were actually in the Bible. The story is so familiar that perhaps it has a life of its own. It's one of the better-known passages in the book of Judges – because in among the narratives of the individual judges over Israel, there are pretty horrific episodes to tackle. The Church of England lectionary – the programme of Bible readings through the year – misses out most of Judges, so we might rarely hear it preached. Usually, when I'm writing these notes, I look for the humour to help tell stories. That's just not been possible this time.

Broadly speaking, Judges tells the story of the Israelites as they take possession of the land promised by God. So we could be forgiven for thinking it ought to reflect flourishing, joy and happiness at the fulfilment of a promise. Yet we read horrors of violence, rape and murder. Instead of thriving communities, there is breakdown and families fail. Forced labour makes a frequent appearance, too. It's one of the hardest parts of the Bible to read, and especially so for women who bear the brunt of the failure to do what God commanded.

Yet this is part of Israel's history – and therefore part of our inheritance as Christians. We need to know these stories are there, or we are only partly reading our Bible. So what should we do with these tricky texts? Perhaps we should be reading these more often, not less. Perhaps these objectional stories of failure and indifference give valuable insight into God's sovereignty. They raise questions for us that don't always have simple answers.

Some of us will find the difficult bits too difficult. Statistics tell us that one in four women have experienced violence or sexual assault. It is very likely that, translated into real people, that statistic means a proportion of our readers have lived experience of these things. So please be kind to yourselves if that's you. Give yourself permission to skip those days, read with a friend, take extra time to pray and process.

I pray that if we engage with these readings together, we can find ways to navigate the path between ignoring them and being overwhelmed by them. I hope to show how the overriding message from Judges is that this is not how things should be.

Beginning to go wrong at the beginning

They smashed the Canaanites and the Perizzites. My-Master-Bezek ran, but they gave chase and caught him. They cut off his thumbs and big toes. (MSG)

It is a skill in this age of fake news and social media to be able to spot when a story isn't all that it seems, isn't it? We might get drawn in by an apparently sensational article, only to discover that the facts are exaggerated. Sometimes we might notice that the story doesn't quite add up, or that there are things missing. I think our reading of the first few chapters of Judges feels a bit like this. We're expecting it to be the story of the settling of the nation under God. We begin with apparent victories and territorial gains. We learn of the death of Joshua – but where's the next leader? There's no one named to step into his shoes. We go straight into battles – but where's the mention of the covenant? We've been told already that God has given the land into the hand of Israel – how come we have continuous fighting for it? Something isn't right. This isn't the story we think it is. We are at a crucial point in Israel's history, but the narrative isn't going to go where we expected.

There are subtle signs. The Benjaminites haven't driven out all the Jebusites. The treatment of My-Master-Bezek is one of them, and it caught my eye. When defeated, he wasn't killed outright – which is what the laws of Deuteronomy said should happen (Deuteronomy 7:2). Instead, My-Master-Bezek was subject to the same humiliating mutilation that he had meted out to his enemies. Why did Judah do something that was a Canaanite punishment? Were the people already so assimilated into the land that they had forgotten the law already? Had they forgotten God had promised them this land if they stuck with his commandments?

'Obediently live by his rules and commands which I'm giving you today so that you'll live well and your children after you – oh, you'll live a long time in the land that God, your God, is giving you.' (Deuteronomy 4:40, MSG)

SARA BATTS-NEALE

Failing memories

But when the judge died, the people went right back to their old ways – but even worse than their parents! – running after other gods, serving and worshipping them. (MSG)

I'm old enough to have begun buying music on vinyl records. That makes me old enough to remember CDs when they were new technology and marketed as virtually indestructible. No longer would we have to listen to a scratched record, jumping back to the same place over and over again. I was reminded of the frustrations of a damaged record when reading Judges 2! The chapter summarises the theological theme of the whole book – how God and God's actions are understood. It's like a stuck record, repeating the same thing over and over again: the Israelites forget the covenant and disobey God; there are consequences; they cry out to God; all is reconciled; then the Israelites forget or ignore the covenant again. Again and again, the cycle of behaviour continues. God is forgotten, until the consequences are felt.

God made a covenant with Israel – if they obeyed his voice and kept his covenant, the people would be his treasured possession, a holy nation (Exodus 19). They're reminded of this by an angel in today's reading (v. 1). This reminder appears to have an effect – the people weep and sacrifice. And for a generation, all is well. But when the memory of Joshua's leadership fades, so does knowledge of the Lord. How can they hope to obey their master's voice when they've simply stopped listening?

Exodus tells the story of Israel escaping slavery, being led by God and depending on him (although not without plenty of grumbling along the way). Judges tells us again and again that the people were enslaved, the exodus reversed. As the saying goes, those that fail to learn from history are doomed to repeat it.

Heavenly Father, I long to keep listening to you. Help me to stay close to you, open to you and learning from you. Amen

SARA BATTS-NEALE

Othniel, the first judge

But when the Israelites cried out to the Lord, the Lord raised up a deliverer for the Israelites, who delivered them, Othniel son of Kenaz, Caleb's younger brother. (NRSV)

The idea that adversity is a test from God can often be a source of real harm – a way of neatly explaining away the inexplicable pain or grief that some of us have to face. Paul tells us in 1 Corinthians 10 that God won't test us beyond our strength. So does that mean that if we can't cope, we're failing as a Christian? Does God really cause harm, to see how we react? That doesn't describe the God that I love and trust – it doesn't feel like a just, merciful and loving God to me.

According to today's reading, the reason other nations were allowed to stay in Canaan was to test the Israelites. Would the Israelites be led astray or would they be true to the commandments? Well, we're only on day three of our exploration of Judges but I suspect you may be able to guess the answer already. They were tempted away from the covenant. They intermarried, and they worshipped other gods. This is the first time we're told exactly what it was that was evil in God's sight. The consequence? Eight years of servitude under King Cushan-rishathaim of Aram-naharaim, followed by Othniel, the first judge. Othniel defeated King Cushan-rishathaim, and the land had rest for 40 years.

Compared to later judges, Othniel is merely a bitpart, a walk-on actor. He receives the spirit of the Lord, but we don't know much else about him. There's a war, but no detail of battles or casualties – just the crucial note that the victory was because the Lord's hand was at work. As we continue our reading in the days to come, we will note how this kind of statement – a victory because God was at work – becomes rarer. We will see how life was oriented away from God, and the dire consequences deepen.

Loving God, we are so prone to temptation. Help us notice where we choose things that take us away from your love and your promises. Amen

SARA BATTS-NEALE

Ehud and Eglon

So [the servants] waited until they were embarrassed. When he still did not open the doors of the roof-chamber, they took the key and opened them. (NRSV)

After Othniel, the land was at rest for another generation – 40 years. Then the pattern repeats: Israel turned away from God and that led to 18 years of servitude under King Eglon of Moab. For the second time, we read that the cries of the people were heard, and a new deliverer was raised up. Ehud is chosen by the Israelites to pay tribute to the king. This kind of tribute wasn't a freely given offering, reflecting willing praise. It was an instrument of oppression.

It's likely that the cool roof chamber was King Eglon's bathroom. So he's attacked at a most vulnerable moment. We get a pretty graphic description of the ambush and Eglon's death – I hope you're not put off your breakfast!

This is a very human story, I think. No one bothered to search for Ehud – did they think he was too insignificant to be effective? Pride in our invincibility often leads to a fall. It is easy to imagine the shuffling embarrassment of the king's servants – not wanting to disturb him, instead waiting until they were completely uncomfortable. In their awkward patience, they allowed Ehud to escape and thus command the rebellion leading to the subjugation of Moab under Israel.

Ehud's preparation – hiding a small sword – and his ability to deceive lead to victory. I wonder if, like me, you find the deception troubling. I suppose I want my conquering heroes to be authentically good – and holy – if they're biblical heroes. This story blurs the idea of things either being good or bad – there is good that comes out of apparent bad. Very often in our lives we long for certainties – for things to be black or white. It can be a challenge when real life presents us instead with varying shades of grey.

How do you deal with uncertainty and the knowledge that we're all a mix of good and bad? When there's only uncertainty, where do you turn for clarity?
SARA BATTS-NEALE

Deborah, the fourth judge

[Deborah] used to sit under the palm of Deborah between Ramah and Bethel in the hill country of Ephraim; and the Israelites came up to her for judgement. (NRSV)

I wonder if you are able to name a female judge. The star of the US reality TV show *Judge Judy* might spring to mind, or maybe another US Supreme Court judge, the late Ruth Bader Ginsburg. Lady Hale, whose rulings (and brooches) rose to prominence in the UK during the Brexit negotiations, might be another. At the time of writing, all bar one judge in the UK's Supreme Court are men, so it's not surprising if the names of our female judges don't come easily to us. It's all the more important, then, that Deborah is introduced in chapter 4 without fanfare or equivocation. We're just told she was a prophetess, that she was married and where she could be found.

Her influence and reputation were sufficient for Barak to lead 10,000 warriors against the commander of the Canaanite army. Her confidence in God's word was sufficient to lead the army with Barak. She gave the order for attack, and Sisera's army was routed.

There aren't many women in the Old Testament in positions of power. It is rare for a woman to be named, and it is rare for a woman to lead quite so decisively. We have to look hard for women's stories in the Bible – they rarely take centre stage in the narratives.

'Behind every great man there's a great woman,' so the saying goes. This story in Judges 4 might be one of the earliest to prove that often the great woman is up front and leading – and that's her rightful, God-given place. Deborah is a name to remember when we need inspiration and confidence. A name to remember if we're told we should know our place. That place may well be leading an army into battle!

God of equity, we pray for all those who fight for justice. We pray for all women still waiting for their voices to be heard and those whose voices are drowned out by others. Amen

SARA BATTS-NEALE

Jael, an impromptu judge

Then, as Barak came in pursuit of Sisera, Jael went out to meet him, and said to him, 'Come, and I will show you the man whom you are seeking.' (NRSV)

It's quite likely that at least one of you reading this can recall a time when you've not been expected to think for yourself. It's frustrating, isn't it, when our knowledge or expertise is sidelined.

I don't think Sisera expected Jael to be able to think for herself. Barak's warriors, under Deborah's leadership, destroyed Sisera's more technologically advanced army. Sisera has fled to what he thinks is friendly territory – Jael's tent. Initially, she responds to his thirst and his need for rest. Then her actions with a tent peg fulfil Deborah's prophecy that Sisera would die at the hand of a woman – seen to be a disgraceful death. (Note how in Judges 9:54 Abimelek asks to be killed by the sword rather than a woman's actions. We look at the first part of that story on Sunday.) Jael's tent peg is part of the means by which God subdues the Israelite's oppressor, allowing them to ultimately destroy King Jabin of Canaan. One school of thought is that Jael should not have violated the rules of hospitality by attacking a man as he slept. On the other hand, Jael's hospitality and protection is demanded by Sisera, rather than being freely given, so perhaps the rules of hospitality should not apply.

How do you feel about Jael? She's not often talked about. This particular act of violence can feel objectionable to our modern sensibilities, perhaps because it is described in such detail. I wonder how you read it in comparison with Eglon's story, who also killed someone as they were vulnerable. I think on balance I would celebrate Jael, even if I'd never want to be in a place where my life depended on repeating her actions. Israel's history – even the unpleasant parts – is not only the history of men. So, when there are women given speaking parts, we really need to notice them.

Lord God, we give you thanks for our capacity to learn, reason and use our intelligence. Give us confidence in our ability to act and help those who would diminish our talents to understand our value as you do. Amen

SARA BATTS-NEALE

Celebrating victory

Villagers in Israel would not fight; they held back until I, Deborah, arose, until I arose, a mother in Israel. (NIV)

There are certain songs that appear to have the power of time travel, aren't there? Music that powerfully reminds us of important moments and precious friends. Indie tunes from the 1990s can transport me back to my student days, making me forget menopause symptoms and making me feel young again. Music helps us create community and is the soundtrack to a shared history.

Today's reading is a song of praise, retelling the narrative of war and Sisera's demise. This kind of song or poem would have been written afterwards, reflecting on the past events. Where was God in all this? He is in the music, drawing the community together in song about victory and becoming the soundtrack to the shared history of God's people.

Interestingly, I've spent quite a long time trying to write about Deborah's use of the first person. I find myself hedging my ideas. Is she claiming credit for her actions? I wonder why I'd be critical of that, given that on Thursday I was urging us to pay attention to her! This is definitely a song of praise to God – it is not less so because Deborah speaks of her part in it. I wonder whether any of us have experienced doubt at taking credit for a job well done, for leading, for taking up space? As a priest, I believe completely in the ability of women to lead within the church and in other spheres of life too, but I work alongside those who don't view my ordination as valid. I wonder whether I'm conditioned to over-apologise for verses like verse 7, which show women in strong positions of power. Does that ring a bell with you, too?

Glory belongs to you, O God. Help us remember that we are made in your image, and let us give thanks for the gifts and talents you have given us to use in your service. Amen

SARA BATTS-NEALE

Where is God?

'But today you have revolted against my father's family. You have murdered his seventy sons on a single stone and have made [Abimelek], the son of his female slave, king over the citizens of Shechem.' (NIV)

Out running one morning somewhere new, I was curious about an intriguing path. Alas, it was a dead end. To make matters worse, I tangled with a bramble and injured both shin and dignity. Brambles are not my favourite plant!

After Gideon's death, God was promptly and comprehensively forgotten. Israel took yet another step away from potential prosperity towards a chaotic and broken land. (If you want to know more about Gideon, take a look at the September–December 2021 issue.)

Abimelek represents something of that chaos. He is a son of Gideon and an unnamed concubine. He's different from Gideon's other sons. He finds a place in Shechem among his mother's relations who support his plan to become king. Abimelek begins his campaign by murdering all but one of his half-brothers.

When this survivor, Jotham, hears of Abimelek's coronation, he shouts a fable at the people of Shechem. It sounds prophetic, but there's one problem – where is God? There's no mention of Abimelek transgressing against *God*. Jotham instead refers to the disloyalty shown to Gideon, his father.

Mount Gerizim was the place of blessing – of the territory and peace that should have been Israel's (Deuteronomy 11:29). Olive trees, fig trees and grapevines represent blessing. Brambles, on the other hand, are invasive, tenacious and have sharp thorns. Not necessarily what we first think of when we think of a king.

This also reminded me of the parable of the sower (Matthew 13); I imagined brambles as one of the plants choking the seeds' growth. In our daily lives, our habits of prayer and seeking God's presence can be stifled when other concerns take over; we can fail to notice our blessings and become complacent. Today's story reminds us to keep God at the centre of our lives.

How easy or hard is it for you to keep God at the centre – to acknowledge his blessings on us and to trust him? It's a life's work for most of us. Ask God for help today.

SARA BATTS-NEALE

Jephthah and a foolish vow

'I have opened my mouth to the Lord, and I cannot take back my vow.'
(NRSV)

Yesterday, brambles represented a way in which all is not well in Israel; today, we have a very specific example of the problem. Male pride and foolishness come to the fore in a story that might leave us baffled but which shows us the power of female community and storytelling in the midst of death.

Jephthah, amid military success, makes a rash vow. Why would he suggest a person as a burnt offering? Surely, there's no expectation of such acts for God's people. We know the story of Abraham and Isaac, where Abraham's faithfulness is put to the test. Isaac isn't sacrificed. It's not God's plan. Has Jephthah muddled his gods? Why does God accept the promise? It certainly sits in contrast with the God we read of elsewhere, who can seemingly be persuaded to change his mind – for example, when Abraham pleads with God on behalf of the righteous in Genesis 18. It reads more in common with the rash promise of the drunken Herod in Matthew 14, offering the daughter of Herodias anything she wanted. He couldn't back down either, even when the girl's request was the cause of the death of John the Baptist.

Women stop being safe when communities aren't working properly. This isn't what God intended for his people. Male pride and false honour – should these things really have a higher value than a daughter's life? Notice how the daughter isn't given a name.

Yet she, and her companions, begin a custom of lament. There is power in that community of women, to bear witness to the abuse that others suffer. We have a part to play too in speaking up and speaking out, claiming our right to live in safe places and seeking justice.

Loving God, we hold before you today all women and girls who are vulnerable and in danger. We thank you for those who campaign for an end to violence against women. Amen

SARA BATTS-NEALE

Judging who's in the in-crowd

They said to him, 'Then say Shibboleth', and he said, 'Sibboleth', for he could not pronounce it right. (NRSV)

A fierce battle rages between Ephraim and Gilead. The Gileadites stop the defeated Ephraimites fleeing across the river Jordan by asking each to pronounce a word that they knew included the 'sh' sound the Ephraimites could not pronounce. And thus the word 'shibboleth' comes into use – a linguistic way to discriminate between different groups of people, and an idea that has been used across the centuries.

Sometimes it's a way to show who's a local and who's a tourist. In Oxford, for example, 'Magdalen' is said differently depending on whether you're talking about a college or a street.

Accents are a way we judge people, too, aren't they? I wonder if you've ever made assumptions about someone's education based on the way they speak. I'm from Essex. A former boss thought it hilarious to deride the way I spoke as Estuary English!

I think we tend to know who the people in our 'tribe' are – like-minded folk, ones we won't be threatened by. We use all sorts of other ways to decide if people are in or out. Some of our churches can be awful places for cliques, for judging others' language about faith and deciding if they're 'proper Christians' or not when it's only for God to know someone's heart. And unless we've led a particularly charmed life, most of us will have experienced the pain of being seen as 'the other' in some way.

We might not put people to the sword for saying a word wrong, but in what ways might we cause people pain by excluding them? Can we be honest with ourselves about the biases we have towards certain kinds of people?

Have you ever felt excluded? It can be painful to be kept outside a friendship group, a church clique or workplace camaraderie. Tell God how you feel. Ask him to show you where you really do belong.

SARA BATTS-NEALE

The arrival of Samson, the twelfth judge

The woman gave birth to a son. They named him Samson. The boy grew and God blessed him. (MSG)

Today's story almost feels like a quiet interlude in the midst of war and disorder, although it's not really going so well – the Israelites are back in another 40 years of servitude, this time under the Philistines.

And then we have a birth narrative. I wonder if you're the same as me – when I think about biblical birth stories I go first to Mary, Hannah or Sarah; I don't really place Samson's mother on that roster of angel-visited women. But that's the territory we are in today – a visitation, a barren woman being blessed, a boy growing. People coming close to God by his angels. It's all there, isn't it?

The detail that I found a bit annoying is how Manoah seems to need to hear from the angel himself. I don't want to resort to stereotypes (particularly after challenging our biases yesterday), but I suspect we all know men who need to know for themselves, disregarding what we tell them. Manoah wants an encounter with God all of his own and asks the angel what they should do for the boy. I do like the way the angel essentially says, 'I've already told your wife', which rather reinforces the idea that the revelation was for her, not her husband. But look – there's something else here. Mary, Hannah, Sarah – do we see the difference? Samson's mother has no name. Just like Jephthah's daughter. There's only one woman named in the remainder of the book of Judges, and that's Delilah (more on her tomorrow).

Just like our first reading last Sunday, these details help us to notice that things aren't as they should be. We are primed to see the trouble ahead for Samson as he grows into the role of Nazirite judge.

Lord God, help us trust in your revelations to us. Help us to see where your word is important for us today. Amen

SARA BATTS-NEALE

Samson's downfall

So Delilah said to Samson, 'Please tell me what makes your strength so great, and how you could be bound, so that one could subdue you.' (NRSV)

A man lusts after women. He visits prostitutes. He falls in love with a woman who does not reciprocate, but instead betrays him for money. He is blinded, she is not remorseful, and he wreaks his revenge by killing several thousand people.

That's not the version of Samson and Delilah we learnt in Sunday school. We almost certainly skipped over the part where Samson first went to a prostitute. We probably didn't pay too much attention to the way Samson is described as loving Delilah, in contrast to all the other women he has been with. We know there's a lesson here somewhere – but what is it?

Verse 17 is the key. Samson, finally giving in to Delilah's demands, tells her the secret of his strength. It's in his hair. He is a Nazirite – even though there are hints throughout the story that he has not lived in the way of holiness that was determined for him (see Numbers 6 for the rules he should have followed). What he forgets, and perhaps didn't even realise, is that his strength is God-given. So, the lesson isn't about pride, being deceitful, peer pressure, obeying your parents or not nagging to get what you want. It's about forgetting that God is God of everything. Samson's strength came from God.

Our strength might not topple buildings, but the strength we have to get through our days is from God. Directly, perhaps, through prayer and our awareness of his presence. Indirectly, through the people God puts in our lives who show us love and care when we need it.

'God is our refuge and strength, a very present help in trouble' (Psalm 46:1).
SARA BATTS-NEALE

Vile outrage

'Has such a thing ever happened since the day that the Israelites came up from the land of Egypt until this day? Consider it, take counsel, and speak out.' (NRSV)

Every year on International Women's Day, Jess Phillips MP reads a list of women who have been killed by men in the preceding twelve months. It is a sobering listen. Like Bori, the student I knew who was murdered last year, many names didn't make the headlines.

Today and tomorrow's readings are troubling. I've prayed much as I have drafted and redrafted thoughts on these verses. They strike us right at the heart of what it is to be a woman. There is no escaping the knowledge that we as women are vulnerable.

The important thing to hold in our minds as we read these difficult passages is that this is not how things are supposed to be. This is not an ordered society. The people are deaf to God. There are names for places, but not people. There is no hospitality – 'Nobody has offered to take me in' (v. 18). An incomer's kindness breaks down in the face of the demands of the local men.

Unnamed women are offered as sacrifices in the place of men. The Levite's concubine is raped to death. There's no decent burial – instead she is dismembered, and her body parts scattered as a warning.

This is ghastly. Because this story is rarely preached about, there is something incredibly shocking when we discover this story for ourselves. But it is there. The story is there, on the page, for us to read. It challenges us, who may ourselves be living with memories of violence and assault, to find a way to live in a broken society. Our faith is not lived in a perfect world. How might we consider it, take counsel and speak out?

Lord, when we are outraged and afraid, may we know your comfort. When we are hurting, may we know your healing. Amen

SARA BATTS-NEALE

No happy ending

In those days there was no king in Israel; all the people did what was right in their own eyes. (NRSV)

Today is the last day of our study of Judges. The gradual disintegration of social order has unfolded, highlighted in the episodes of violence, betrayal, death and destruction. It hasn't been a pleasant fortnight's readings, and I'm afraid there isn't a happy ending to wrap up with. The last episode tells of more slaughter and the casual abduction of women in order to provide wives for the tribe of Benjamin.

We are left, as we have been on so many days this past two weeks, with a sense of the vulnerability of women. Perhaps we are angry – at the parallels we see in our headlines today as well as at the fate of these women thousands of years ago. Maybe you're wondering why these narratives were included in the Bible at all. How might we reconcile these episodes with the idea of all scripture being inspired by God (2 Timothy 3:16)? Those are all legitimate reactions to have. If you've wanted to throw these Bible notes out of the window, trust me that's also legitimate. This has been a hard set to write – to keep us walking with God even as we consider the result of other's failures to do so.

I think verse 25 sums it up. There is no king, no wise ruler to listen to God, to shape a community, to speak to the people of the covenant. Everyone does what is right in their own eyes. A warning to us all to rely not on our own judgements, but always to test our assumptions and ideas against the scripture and teaching we can access. And most of all, to stay close to God.

'He has told you, O mortal, what is good; and what does the Lord require of you but to do justice, and to love kindness, and to walk humbly with your God?' (Micah 6:8)

SARA BATTS-NEALE

How to break the worry habit

Bridget Plass writes:

Maybe it isn't a coincidence that I was asked to write these notes at a time when there has been a huge amount to worry about both in the world and in my own life. But then it was ever thus! Jesus told his disciples that he was not asking his Father to take them out of the world or to give them a problem-free ride (John 17:15). Let's face it, there have always been wars and pandemics that decimate populations, family crises and situations that threaten to devour hope and confidence. Yet Jesus tells us it is pointless to worry: 'Can any one of you by worrying add a single hour to your life?… Therefore do not worry about tomorrow, for tomorrow will worry about itself. Each day has enough trouble of its own' (Matthew 6:27, 34, NIV).

Does this mean we are living in sin if we get anxious? Some people think so. I remember a talk where we were told that not worrying was a command. How many of the congregation went home that day in despair, maybe worrying about what is left in the food cupboard or how they will afford school uniforms, thinking secretly that birds and wildflowers have a few less pressures or that Jesus couldn't know what it would be like to live in the 21st century.

There is no silver bullet that will easily solve this problem but there are two things that might be worth considering. The first is a determination to be truthful with God and with each other. The centre of Jesus' message, recorded in both Matthew and Luke, is that staying close to our heavenly Father will prevent us from being overwhelmed by the cares of this world. *Love* of money is the root of all evil, not the money itself. Feeding the worry habit, prioritising material security and forgetting that God's undeserved kindness has given us the kingdom is also dangerous. The second is to take any and every opportunity to gently laugh at not only our tendency to worry but also the way in which we worry about worry!

God, are you listening?

Do not be anxious about anything, but in every situation, by prayer and petition, with thanksgiving, present your requests to God. (NIV)

Are we supposed to genuinely thank God for every single situation we find ourselves in? 'Thank you, God, that someone I love is dying'; 'Thank you that the world is in turmoil and people are getting badly hurt.' Are we supposed to beat ourselves up for not feeling at all thankful or for feeling anxious? Surely not!

When our eldest son was about three, we were staying with a couple who had an expectation that the rituals of correct procedure should always be carried out. We told him that it was important to say thank you when we left for home, and we practised so it could be done perfectly. On the doorstep he politely uttered, 'Thank you very much for having me.' Unfortunately, it was followed a mini-second's pause later with, 'There, that's got that done.' Ring any bells?

Experience shows that our requests to God are not always answered in the way we would like, however correctly we ask. Yet understanding today's verses is crucial to our relationship with our Father God. I firmly believe that the true reading means giving thanks that we have a God who is completely approachable. We don't need to worry that our requests and our prayers will be criticised, mocked or deemed incorrectly worded. Jesus asked that the children should be allowed to come to him, and it's the same Jesus who said to Philip: 'Anyone who has seen me has seen the Father' (John 14:9).

Jesus, you promised that when we close the door to the world and tell our Father everything that is on our minds he will listen. Help us to believe this as much as we believe in you. Amen

BRIDGET PLASS

When we need reassurance

The peace of God, which transcends all understanding, will guard your hearts and your minds in Christ Jesus… Jesus came and stood among them and said, 'Peace be with you'… Then he said to Thomas, 'Put your finger here; see my hands. Reach out your hand and put it into my side. Stop doubting and believe.' (NIV)

In his letter to the Philippians, Paul teaches us that if we come to God trusting that our problems will be removed, even though the promised answer may not be exactly what we hoped for, there is a greater gift in store for us. It's something money can't buy, and it isn't the result of advanced medical science or technology. In fact, it is something that doesn't make any sense at all in worldly terms. This is the peace that passes all understanding, that keeps our hearts and minds in the knowledge and love of God.

When the risen Jesus appeared through a locked door, the first thing he said to his terrified friends was, in the words of Corporal Jones, 'Don't panic!' – or rather 'Peace be with you.' But what if you don't feel the peace, if your inability to accept this invisible gift makes you feel even more panicky and therefore more of a failure than you did before? Maybe all of us have felt like that at some point in our lives. So, thank you, Jesus, that yet again you showed gentle understanding that some of the more fragile among us need physical reassurance; that some of us have had easy trust in words eroded by our life experience. And thank you for the times when we are given the privilege to stand in for you, to be your arms to envelope those who need the promise of peace to be accompanied by a hug.

Dear Jesus, give us your eyes and ears so that we can pass on a little of your gift of peace when someone most needs it. Amen

BRIDGET PLASS

A waste of days

'Be careful, or your hearts will be weighed down with carousing, drunkenness and the anxieties of life, and that day will close on you suddenly like a trap.' (NIV)

My dad was a good man and a faithful churchgoer all his life. He worked in the local bank. Not wealthy, not a carouser and definitely not a drunkard, he was nonethless constantly burdened by cares of the world – his world. His faith was based on the maxim 'God helps those who help themselves', which meant he enjoyed few, if any, of the free gifts of abundant life.

He was a habitual worrier, weighed down with what he saw as his responsibilities, so much so that when he and my mother decided to buy a summerhouse for the garden – somewhere to relax in – security caused him huge anxiety. His solution was bizarre. The key to the summerhouse hung on a hook in his locked garage. The key to the garage was in a drawer in the kitchen. The key to the kitchen drawer was on a ring he kept with him. By the time they actually got into their garden retreat, the weather often took a turn for the worse and the whole locking procedure had to be reversed.

Worrying about what might happen to every aspect of his life, finances and family frequently robbed him of sleep. Retirement and grandchildren brought moments of the joy promised by Jesus and released him from the trap he had fallen into. Dementia loosened once and for all the reins of responsibility, and it was an unfettered child in his 90s who sang old familiar hymns, dreamed in his garden and finally forgot to worry. Such a waste of years. And maybe a warning for us to refuse to let worry dominate every hour of every day!

Dear Father God, we are sorry for wasting the precious time given to us by worrying about what might happen instead of living each day as it comes. Help us to trust in your goodness. Amen

BRIDGET PLASS

More than a badge

'I will ask the Father, and he will give you another advocate to help you and be with you forever – the Spirit of truth'… The Spirit helps us in our weakness. We do not know what we ought to pray for, but the Spirit himself intercedes for us through wordless groans. (NIV)

Badges are part of modern life. Name badges are sewn on to school clothes late into the night before a new school term begins. Badges for achievements are proudly displayed on the sleeves of uniformed groups such as Cubs and Scouts, Brownies and Guides. Some badges represent military achievements and honour. Others can be collectable, representing places we have explored. Badges at conferences identify us to our fellow attendees. But when did the gifts of the Spirit become visible badges of honour indicating that we have achieved full spiritual status as followers of Christ? Some people have misinterpreted Paul's teaching in 1 Corinthians 12 and this has caused pain and worry as the misunderstanding has taken root.

As a newish Christian I remember I was actually put on the spot as to which specific spiritual gift I had been given. All my insecurities immediately went into overdrive. I didn't speak in tongues at the time. I certainly didn't prophesy. I wish I had known then how far away this thinking was from the original intention voiced with passion by Jesus, all too aware how tough it was going to be once he was no longer around. He knew that his followers, both then and now, would need a trustworthy friend, a Spirit of truth to strengthen and give courage, enabling God to meet us halfway and bring comfort when our distress robs us of words; a friend to speak for us even more effectively that Aaron did for Moses.

The Spirit of truth is not a visible add-on or a prize for achievement, but a dear companion making sure that we don't lose touch with our Father even when life chokes us up.

Dear Father God, today help me to genuinely open my heart and allow the Holy Spirit to take all my tumbling pain and thoughts that will not form into words and give them to you. Amen

BRIDGET PLASS

Help! I think I'm lost

'My Father's house has many rooms; if that were not so, would I have told you that I am going there to prepare a place for you?... You know the way to the place where I am going.' Thomas said to him, 'Lord, we don't know where you are going, so how can we know the way?' (NIV)

I hate getting lost – almost as much as I hate being late. I admit my stress levels soar out of control on long journeys as I face unexpected traffic jams or road diversions. Even the arrival of the satnav hasn't completely solved the problem.

Recently we set off on a long, quite familiar journey and were about to take our normal route when the satnav informed us that there were major problems on the motorway so we would be rerouted. Fine, we thought, until we were led blindly through apparently never-ending windy, ridiculously narrow country roads and town after town with the inevitably frequent pedestrian traffic lights and traffic blockages. We had absolutely no idea where we were or even which county we were in. Our satnav appeared to have lost the plot completely. Our three-and-a-half-hour journey took seven hours and we arrived frazzled, tired and, yes, you guessed it, late.

Our lives, and I suspect yours too, have included periods when we have found ourselves in an unknown territory and felt totally lost, rerouted by unexpected crises on our life journey. We can end up feeling harassed and angry, let down by the God who we trusted to do a better job in navigating our route through life.

I came across a letter written by C.S. Lewis in which he used the analogy of rowing to explain guidance. The rowers are seated with their backs facing the way ahead, dependent on the helmsman to steer safely. He warns of the consequences of worrying about the way ahead. If the rower is constantly looking over their shoulder to check the route, they can end up going round in circles.

Father God, help me to allow you to be my helmsman today, so that wherever my journey takes me, I can keep my eyes on you and trust you know where we are heading. Amen

BRIDGET PLASS

Time to take a stand

Whenever Hannah went up to the house of the Lord, her rival provoked her till she wept and would not eat. Her husband Elkanah would say to her, 'Hannah, why are you weeping? Why don't you eat?'… Hannah stood up. (NIV)

Hannah's anxiety and desperation at not being able to bear Elkanah a child coupled with Peninnah's bullying meant that the yearly pilgrimage to Shiloh had become a nightmare for her. Hannah finally makes a stand and from that moment her life changes. The Holy Spirit does not want us to become doormats for the world to walk over. Allowing worry and anxiety to grow unabated can make us feel powerless and paralysed. Hannah stood up. In the temple, she bravely challenges Eli's false presumption that her crying out to God in anguish means she is drunk. She leaves the temple with his blessing.

While he has now passed away, I loved my father. He loved me, but his desire for me to succeed meant that I inevitably disappointed him. School reports caused annual panic; my worst mark seized upon with a demand for explanation. Even in adulthood, I felt set to fail. One morning, shortly after coming to stay with us, he came in from the garden tutting and shaking his head over a long list of things I should have done. Something broke. I stood up. 'Come on,' I said firmly, taking his arm and shepherding him through the door. 'This bare patch is where your grandsons love to play cricket. These delphiniums may look a bit feeble, but I grew them from seed. I didn't prune the roses because we all love the amazing shapes they make in the old, gnarled apple trees which you think we should have cut down.'

Determinedly, I steered him round the colourful semi-wilderness that was our beloved back garden, and, in the end, he was chuckling. The old anxieties and worries didn't disappear, but something in me had changed.

'For the Spirit God gave us does not make us timid, but gives us power, love and self-discipline' (2 Timothy 1:7). Is there something God is waiting for you to take a stand about? Make a start today.

BRIDGET PLASS

You know my weaknesses

The Lord turned to him and said, 'Go in the strength you have and save Israel'... That same night the Lord said to him... 'Tear down your father's altar to Baal and cut down the Asherah pole beside it'... So Gideon... did as the Lord told him. But because he was afraid of his family and the townspeople, he did it at night. (NIV)

Maybe one of the greatest worries most of us share is that when the crunch comes, we won't be strong enough or brave enough to do whatever it is God calls us to do. We think we know ourselves too well. We sometimes forget that God knows us even better.

Gideon received the order: 'Go in the strength you have' (v. 14). He did exactly that. He didn't have a lot of courage. He was terrified of what would happen when those close to him discovered he had dared to carry out God's orders. So, what did he do? Wanting to be obedient, he took his little capsule of courage and tore down Baal's temple in the night. And God was fine about that. How easy it is for us to look at a task that is staring us in the face and, because we worry that we are not strong enough or brave enough to do it exceptionally well, decide it can't possibly have our name on it. It could be a visit, reading the lesson in church, standing up for something you believe in, confronting someone who you believe is wrong or taking a stand against evil.

Facing our fears (and let's face it, Gideon's worry was well placed), accepting our limitations and doing our best are probably also fine with God. In Gideon's case, it was the first step towards believing he could be braver next time. Maybe the same will be true for us.

Dear Father, thank you for reminding us that you know us through and through. Help us to be prepared to do our very best whatever turns out to be the next challenge you give us. Amen

BRIDGET PLASS

What to say

Anxiety weighs down the heart, but a kind word cheers it up. (NIV)

I am quite sure that when the writer of this proverb asserts that a kind word will have the effect of cheering up the heart, he did not mean 'Chin up' or 'Cheer up, it'll probably never happen'! When have comments like those ever helped anyone? They are usually designed to remove pressure from the observer who is uncomfortable in the presence of someone who is creating a gloomy atmosphere. Even 'I know exactly how you feel', intended to express empathy, often has the effect of minimising the unique grief and anxiety being experienced.

The more we understand the heart of God, the more we will recognise the role we need to embrace in reaching out to those he loves with sensitivity and genuine compassion. God so loved the world – and every human being without exception comes from God and is loved by God with an incomprehensible love. As our love and understanding of the heart of God grows, the more the suffering of those we meet becomes our own. We mourn with them.

None of us will ever forget TV footage of the extraordinary welcome those fleeing Ukraine received as they crossed borders into neighbouring countries. Language barriers disappeared. Smiles, hugs, toys and cups of tea greeted the exhausted and desperately anxious mothers, children and bewildered elderly who found themselves homeless. Of course, this was only the beginning of finding temporary solutions to complex problems, but the warmth and sympathy represented an understanding of the depth of fear and loss those arriving were experiencing. There was no expectation that they would 'pull themselves together' or 'cheer up'.

Open our hearts, Lord, so that we can avoid simplistic responses to those who are struggling and instead offer genuine kindness and sympathy. Amen
BRIDGET PLASS

Waiting for news

On the seventh day the child died. David's attendants were afraid to tell him that the child was dead, for they thought, 'While the child was still living, he wouldn't listen to us when we spoke to him. How can we now tell him the child is dead? He may do something desperate.' (NIV)

A recent church email asked for prayer for a member 'who continues to battle with pain and anxiety as she waits to hear from her surgeon about an operation date'. Waiting for news can cause a level of anxiety and worry unlike any other. We feel powerless, afraid and our brain goes into overdrive imagining the worst, while trying to hold on to the possibility of the best. It's exhausting, relentless and often sleep-snatching.

I remember the day my husband and I stood in a field putting off the moment of opening a phone message which would tell us the result of an emergency brain MRI scan. That time it was good news. I also remember the day I waited for the hospital consultant to hear whether my mother's pancreatic cancer was terminal. It was. I always felt sorry that he had to give me such devastating news.

My father once described his childhood memory from World War I. The all-too-frequent occasions when a woman whose husband was away fighting opened the door to the postman carrying the black-bordered telegram. How the postman must have dreaded the walk up to the allotted address, almost as much as the homeowner dreaded his arrival.

Many of us may be able to identify with David's agonised waiting, dreading the inevitable while praying desperately for good news. David's behaviour and fasting were so extreme that his servants worried for his sanity if his prayers were not answered. Yet we are told that when David heard his baby was dead, he got up, washed, changed his clothes, went to worship in the temple, then went home and ate a meal. For some of us, as in the case of my hearing what I so didn't want to hear about my mum, a calm can come from acceptance, and letting God help us face the future head on.

Father, we pray today for all those waiting for news. Please give them a sense of your understanding and love. Amen

BRIDGET PLASS

When we know we have failed

Once I was bitter and broken hearted. I was stupid and ignorant, and I treated you as a wild animal would. But I never really left you, and you hold my right hand. Your advice has been my guide, and later you will welcome me in glory. In heaven I have only you, and on this earth you are all I want. (CEV)

Asaph, the writer of this psalm, has been berating himself over his attitude to those who are sailing through their lives having a great time and ignoring God. About such people, Asaph says: 'Their pride is like a necklace, and they commit sin more often than they dress themselves… They sneer and say cruel things, and because of their pride, they make violent threats' (vv. 6, 8). Filled with envy and bitterness, he is hardly behaving in a way befitting the role he has been given by David as writer, musician and worship leader. He is worrying that he has moved many miles away from the man of God he hoped he was.

A good friend of mine spent some time in hospital. He thought he would prove himself to be a worthy disciple of his Lord, strong and fearless, secure in the knowledge that he was a soldier for Christ. Instead, he found himself full of self-pity, grumpy, demanding and tearful, with no sense at all that God was with him. Forlorn, he equated himself with Peter after his denial in the courtyard. He was not at all pleased with himself. What would God think? Could things ever be okay again?

What about us? Are we frozen like rabbits caught in the car headlights, terrified that our failures have separated us from God's love forever? The story of Peter reminds us that with God there is always the possibility of a new beginning. And here is Asaph, remembering that even when we mess up and even when we don't understand what is going on, God will still be hanging on to us (v. 23). But can we believe it?

Heavenly Father, help us to believe the truth of verse 23, that 'you hold my right hand', for ourselves and for those we love. Amen

BRIDGET PLASS

When things get tangled

Trust in the Lord with all your heart and lean not on your own understanding; in all your ways submit to him, and he will make your paths straight. (NIV)

Many years ago, my husband Adrian wrote a piece in which the speaker talks about the many things causing her to be anxious. She starts with tiny worries, such as whether she should be eating meat, then moves on to whether the increasingly clunking noises made by her car will mean huge garage bills. Then her worry and fear spirals further to the possibility of imminent nuclear war. The result is an overwhelming tangled heap of fear and worry that means she can't think straight: 'Still, the night they drop the bomb I suppose I'll get some sleep at last' (from the poem 'Stress' in *Clearing Away the Rubbish* by Adrian Plass, Zondervan, 2000).

The piece is frighteningly relevant as I write these notes. The news is full of scary realities – the Covid pandemic, climate change, the invasion of Ukraine and threats from yet another power-mad leader. Whatever might be in the news as you read these notes, I imagine feelings of total helplessness won't be far away.

We can, of course, make our contribution to recycling and reduced plastic use, but we can't change the situation our world finds itself in. Many of us are also facing money problems, family crises or health problems that together make our worries impossible to get under control or even face. A first step could be to invite the Holy Spirit into the mess of your anxiety. Lay your jumble of fears out in front of him like a pile of tangled jewellery and ask for his help to gently tease out the threads, separating each piece so that you can clearly identify your worries and see them clearly for what they are.

Father, help us to separate out the worries that are in our control so that we can tackle them one by one and, with your help, reduce the pile to something we can face up to. Amen

BRIDGET PLASS

Nothing can separate us

For I am convinced that neither death nor life, neither angels nor demons… nor anything else in all creation, will be able to separate us from the love of God that is in Christ Jesus our Lord. (NIV)

I am really glad that Paul became convinced that absolutely nothing could separate him from the love of God. Rationally speaking, one might have expected him to be less confident. After all, the three days that Paul was forced to spend in total darkness after meeting Jesus on the road to Damascus must have been full of torment. 'What have I been doing? I have blood on my hands – the blood of Stephen, the blood of followers of Jesus Christ, who has associated my persecution of his followers with personal attack. Surely, I am beyond forgiveness.'

Then came the glorious moment when Ananias put his hand on his shoulder and called him brother, and Paul knew he had not been abandoned. He was not to know at that point that his welcome into his new life in Christ had been placed in the hands of a mere mortal – someone confident enough in his relationship with God to speak plainly, to question whether God was actually aware of what Paul had been doing to his beloved followers.

How easy it is for us to worry about our worthiness, to become so anxious that we secretly question God's wisdom but can't express our doubts to him for fear we will be thrown away. What a relief to be able to tune into the confidence of these two men and relax in the knowledge that they have been there before us. We really don't have to worry that any amount of failure will be able to separate us from God.

Lord Jesus, we have things we need to say. Maybe things we need to do. Please help us to trust your love more. Amen

BRIDGET PLASS

When it all gets too much

'Come to me, all you who are weary and burdened, and I will give you rest… For my yoke is easy and my burden is light.'

'Do not be afraid, little flock, for your Father has been pleased to give you the kingdom.' (NIV)

I have a sturdy little toddler grandson who I am all too ready to hand over to his mum if I have been carrying him for any distance. I love the moment of handover not just because it relieves my aching back, but also because I enjoy watching him place his plump sticky hands on his mum's cheeks, squashing his face against hers in total confidence that he loves her, and that he is loved and adored in return.

But I also know how it feels to face handing over a role that has been life-giving or something I felt I could do well, but that now is getting too much for me. Maybe you too know how this feels – the weight of responsibilities bringing us to our knees. Church has been known to add extra weights to those we are already carrying, unaware of the pressure being placed on our shoulders. It's not that we are lazy or that we want to give up; we may even enjoy the work. But sometimes we need to concede that it is too heavy for us to carry any longer.

It's never easy to admit that we are finding things hard and that we are exhausted. Maybe we are afraid we will be judged by folk who will not understand. We may know by heart the phrase 'Perfect love drives out fear' (1 John 4:18), but many of us secretly struggle to relate it to our family or church community, let alone our relationship with Jesus. But here is Jesus calling his followers his 'little flock'. Here is Jesus telling us to come and dump the heavy weight we are carrying and swap it for something he is confident we can manage, not because we have failed but simply because he wants to look after us.

Dear Jesus, I want to come to you. I want to hand over the things that are too heavy for me to carry any longer. Help me to trust in your care. Amen

BRIDGET PLASS

Unexpected blessings

'See how the flowers of the field grow. They do not labour or spin. Yet I tell you that not even Solomon in all his splendour was dressed like one of these. If that is how God clothes the grass of the field, which is here today and tomorrow is thrown into the fire, will he not much more clothe you – you of little faith!' (NIV)

Do you remember when the world stopped moving for many of us at the start of the 2020 Covid pandemic? It was almost as though everything we had known in our busy, noisy lives had fallen under a Sleeping Beauty spell. It was going to be the discovery of a vaccine not the kiss of a prince that would slowly wake the world up from its enforced Covid slumber, and for many this was a time of sadness, worry and isolation. Key workers, especially in the NHS, were having an exhausting and traumatic time, while many parents, confined under the law of lockdown, found homeschooling was an interesting challenge.

But some unexpectedly good things did occur during those many strange months. For a little while we weren't supposed to worry about what we should be doing or where the money was coming from. We actually had time to witness the world around us exploding into the colours of an exceptional spring, to hear nesting birds calling to each other and wonder at tiny, exquisite flowers peeping bravely through the cracks of city pavements or appearing overnight under sheltering trees when we ventured out for our allowed daily walk. Of course, not everyone will have given God the credit, but maybe that didn't matter so very much. The generosity of God's creation has always been for the whole world. It was just a temporary enforced respite, but as I see more children jumping in puddles and laughing at ducks, families choosing to spend time in the beauty of local parks and country lanes, I can't help but feel heaven will be happy that there were at least some advantages to life being put on pause for a little while.

Heavenly Father, thank you for the reminder that your creation, existing in all its wonder, helps all your children, whether they recognise you or not, to clothe their minds with beauty and survive the most frightening of times. Amen
BRIDGET PLASS

In the company of trees

Jackie Harris writes:

I have always loved trees: their shape, blossoms, vibrant colours and rich bounty are a delight. Not being a sun worshipper, I appreciate the cool shade they offer in the summer – and trees can also keep you surprisingly dry when it's wet. On a timed visit to a National Trust estate, when the cafes remained closed due to Covid restrictions, my husband and I were able to take refuge from the rain and enjoy our picnic in relative comfort under a giant redwood tree. And they are ancient – some hundreds of years old. What tales they could tell if they could talk to us!

However, it wasn't until I began this study that I realised trees are everywhere in the Bible. In fact, it is claimed that other than people and God, trees are the most mentioned living thing in the Bible. From the garden of Eden right through to the holy city in Revelation, trees are part of God's story. You will find them in almost all the big events, and they often appear alongside major characters in the Bible. Think of Noah receiving an olive branch, Abraham sitting under the oak at Mamre, Jacob using tree branches to increase his flock and Zacchaeus climbing a tree to see Jesus.

In the books of the prophets and in the psalms, trees are often symbols of strength, endurance, righteousness and provision, as well as images for the blessing and judgement of God. One commentator suggests that we can see how things were going in the relationship between God and his people by what was happening to the trees. 'There will be no figs on the tree, and their leaves will wither', warns Jeremiah, as he urges the people to repent (Jeremiah 8:13, NIV). But if the people were willing to turn back to him, then God's blessing is seen in the provision of healthy trees: 'I will put in the desert the cedar and the acacia, the myrtle and the olive. I will set junipers in the wasteland, the fir and the cypress together' (Isaiah 41:19, NIV).

Moreover, trees are at the heart of the gospel, for Jesus died on a tree for us, securing our freedom from sin and reconciliation with the Father.

As we study a selection of Bible passages featuring trees (and we can only scratch the surface this week), let us thank God for these wonderful creations, which sprang from God's amazing imagination, speaking so powerfully of his love and care for us.

God's abundant generosity

Then God said, 'Let the land produce vegetation: seed-bearing plants and trees on the land that bear fruit with seed in it, according to their various kinds.' (NIV)

We begin at the beginning, when God spoke trees into being on the third day of creation. They came before any other living thing was made. God then gave the trees to Adam and Eve and to 'all the beasts of the earth and all the birds in the sky and all the creatures that move along the ground' (1:30). Everything that had the breath of life in it was to find sustenance from the trees and plants that God had made.

Our first lesson from the trees, then, is to marvel at God's amazing creativity and generosity. There are so many different types of trees: from tall cedars and broad oaks to graceful willows and trees bearing all kinds of fruit, nuts and oils. But trees are more than things of beauty or a source of food; we now know that they are essential to life.

Consider for a moment what trees provide and do for us. The fruit and seeds not only provide food but also have many other uses. Some of the seeds provide oil for cooking and lighting. Some of these oils and some tree barks are used in medicine or in beauty treatments. Wood from trees has been essential in building and construction and, of course, trees provide habitats for various animals, birds and insects. But there's more: trees give us shade, provide windbreaks and even clean the air we breathe! The Woodland Trust says trees are 'the lungs of our cities' because of their ability to remove excess carbon dioxide from the air and convert it into oxygen, and scientists now recognise how vital trees are in the battle against climate change.

Beauty, provision, protection... as the International Tree Foundation says: 'Trees give life and improve livelihoods.' What an amazing gift!

If you can, take a walk among the trees today, thanking God for his provision and care for us.

JACKIE HARRIS

The importance of obedience

The Lord God made all kinds of trees grow out of the ground – trees that were pleasing to the eye and good for food. In the middle of the garden were the tree of life and the tree of the knowledge of good and evil. (NIV)

God has created his beautiful world and the first living being. Now he plants a garden for the man he has created. It's a beautiful garden, the perfect environment for Adam and later Eve. The trees that he causes to grow are both 'pleasing to the eye and good for food' (v. 9). We see again God's provision and care. He gives good and beautiful things for man to enjoy, and he follows this by giving Adam a purpose. He is to work the ground and take care of the trees and all that the garden holds.

But there's something else. God also sets boundaries. There are two special trees in the garden, the tree of life and the tree of the knowledge of good and evil. Adam may eat from any of the other trees, but the fruit of the tree of the knowledge of good and evil is not to be eaten (Genesis 3:22 says Adam was also forbidden to eat from the tree of life, but perhaps such a boundary only came after the initial rebellion in Genesis 2). Adam is warned that the consequences of eating the fruit from the tree of the knowledge of good and evil will be severe.

Why did God put those trees there? We don't know, but we do know what happened when Adam and Eve chose to disobey.

What about us? We may not be living in a paradise, but we have been given many good and beautiful things to enjoy. We also have a purpose – to believe in Jesus and to make him known (John 6:29). What about boundaries? What is God saying to us about what we can or can't do? Will we trust that God knows what is best for us?

The lesson we take from these trees is that God created us to bless us with life and joy, but we can only know that life when we trust him and obey him.

'The Lord says, "I will guide you along the best pathway for your life. I will advise you and watch over you"' (Psalm 32:8, NLT).

JACKIE HARRIS

God is watching

The word of the Lord came to me: 'What do you see, Jeremiah?' 'I see the branch of an almond tree,' I replied. (NIV)

Almond trees were abundant in ancient Syria and Palestine – indeed Anathoth, where Jeremiah lived, is still a centre for growing almonds today. What Jeremiah sees in his first vision is something very ordinary, something he would be very familiar with. I wonder if this was deliberate on God's part to encourage Jeremiah, who was fearful and reluctant to accept his calling as a prophet.

It may well be an example of God's gentleness with those he calls to a specific ministry, but the choice of an almond tree has a deeper significance. There is a play on words which is lost in our English translation, for the Hebrew word for almond sounds like the Hebrew word for watching. God is assuring Jeremiah that he is watching over his word. What God has spoken will come to pass. He has watched his people turn away from him, and now he declares that their actions will have consequences. And the vision of a branch of an almond tree, the first of all the fruit trees to flower, indicates that judgement will come soon.

It was a harsh message to deliver – no wonder Jeremiah was afraid – but Jeremiah would also see God's plan for restoration (chapter 23). God was watching over that word too and was ready to act quickly when his people turned back to him.

The almond tree reminds us of the power of God's word. God spoke the world into being, and his words continue to achieve his purposes. God says in Isaiah: 'My word that goes out from my mouth... will not return to me empty, but will accomplish what I desire' (55:11). We can take God at his word and trust him.

What word has God been speaking to you? Trust that he is watching and will bring it to pass.

JACKIE HARRIS

The blessings of godliness

The righteous will flourish like a palm tree, they will grow like a cedar of Lebanon. (NIV)

So far, we have explored what the trees teach us about God and what he has done for us. Now we turn our attention to what they teach us about the people God wants us to be. Paul says we are to 'put off [our] old self… and to put on the new self, created to be like God in true righteousness and holiness' (Ephesians 4:22–24). So how do we do this? Let's learn from the cedar tree.

Cedars are almost always referenced with admiration in the Bible: they are 'tall and lofty' (Isaiah 2:13), strong and beautiful (Song of Songs 5:15) and fragrant (Hosea 14:6). They are also evergreen. David tells us that a righteous person is like a cedar. The abundant growth, longevity, fragrance and usefulness of the trees is a picture of what our lives could be like if we pursue godliness.

But the cedars don't only teach us what we *could* be like; they also teach us *how* to grow in godliness. When Hosea prophesies of a restored Israel, he says: 'Like a cedar of Lebanon he will send down his roots; his young shoots will grow' (Hosea 14:5–6). I was fascinated to discover that the roots of the cedar tree go down as deep as the tree is high. This is what allows them to grow tall and stately. So, the lesson from the cedar is that if we want to grow in righteousness, we need to be rooted in God's truth. As we study God's word and seek to apply it in our lives, we are putting down roots that will enable us to grow and flourish whatever our age.

'In the way of righteousness there is life; along that path is immortality.'
(Proverbs 12:28).

JACKIE HARRIS

Seeking Jesus

[Zaccheus] wanted to see who Jesus was, but because he was short he could not see over the crowd. So he ran ahead and climbed a sycamore-fig tree to see him. (NIV)

I love the detail Luke gives us in this story. First, he tells us that Zacchaeus is a 'chief tax collector' and wealthy (v. 2). Those few words tell us a lot about Zacchaeus. The job was notorious for corruption and since Luke adds that he was wealthy, we can assume he took every advantage of his position. Second, he wanted to see Jesus, but he had a problem – he was small. He couldn't hope to see over the crowd and his job would have made him very unpopular, so no one was likely to help him.

Zacchaeus, however, is determined, so he runs ahead of the crowds and climbs a tree. Luke tells us it was a sycamore-fig tree. Such trees were common and often planted on roadsides. It's a type of tree that grows to a great height, with large leaves and low branches – so it was perfect for a small man wanting to be able to see while remaining unseen.

However, Zacchaeus doesn't remain unseen, for Jesus not only sees him but also calls him down and then invites himself to stay at Zacchaeus' house.

I think there's both a challenge and a wonderful encouragement in this story. In running ahead of the crowds and climbing a tree, Zacchaeus was prepared to put his dignity aside in order to see Jesus. It's rather an awkward meeting place, but it leads to a life-changing encounter. What might we need to do to enable us to get a clearer sight of Jesus today? And Jesus saw him, even though he was hidden in the tree. When we make the effort to seek out Jesus, we can be sure that we too will be seen by him.

Lord Jesus, thank you that you are always ready to meet with us when we seek you out. Help me to see you today and to know that you see me, whatever my circumstances. Amen

JACKIE HARRIS

What are you made of?

'No good tree bears bad fruit, nor does a bad tree bear good fruit. Each tree is recognised by its own fruit.' (NIV)

Remember the nursery rhyme 'What are little girls made of?' I'm sure we'd all like to think that we are full of 'sugar and spice and all things nice', but these verses challenge us to examine ourselves to see exactly what we're made of.

Jesus has been talking about judging others. We are not to point out other people's failings but consider our own, and these verses continue that theme of self-examination.

What sort of fruit tree are we? Jesus says good things come from the good stored in our hearts, so we must be careful what we allow to take root and grow there. Paul's letter to the Philippians (4:8) has some wise advice about what we should focus on.

How do we know what is in our heart? Jesus indicates that we should listen to what we say: 'For the mouth speaks what the heart is full of' (v. 45). Next time you are chatting to someone in person or on the phone, try listening to yourself. What are the topics of conversation? Are you quick to praise or do you speak negatively? Is there a tendency to grumble or gossip? For many of us, the way we speak to ourselves might be the problem. And how do we speak to God? Do we approach him humbly, with thanksgiving, or do we simply present a list of our concerns? The sobering truth is that the things we say and how we say them reveal the condition and character of our hearts.

Producing good fruit – 'love, joy, peace, forbearance, kindness, goodness, faithfulness, gentleness and self-control' (Galatians 5:22–23) – takes hard work and comes from a heart that has been changed by God. Let's be willing for him to work in us so that we will be good trees bearing good fruit.

'Search me, God, and know my heart; test me and know my anxious thoughts. See if there is any offensive way in me, and lead me in the way everlasting' *(Psalm 139:23–24).*

JACKIE HARRIS

Our future hope

On each side of the river stood the tree of life, bearing twelve crops of fruit, yielding its fruit every month. And the leaves of the tree are for the healing of the nations. (NIV)

Our study of trees brings us to the final chapter of the Bible. Here, in John's awe-inspiring vision of the holy city, we see again the tree of life, but this time it is accessible to all. The curse has been lifted, and God's people are once again in the garden and enjoying God's presence.

And, here in Revelation, there's another difference in the tree. This time it stands on both sides of the river. Some translations have trees either side of the river – indeed some commentators suggest the text indicates a whole grove of trees. Whatever the number, John tells us how varied and available the fruit will be. The trees will yield twelve different kinds of fruit every month. God's provision is new and, as ever, generous.

But that's not all, even the leaves are valuable. God's special life-giving trees are never empty or barren, they always have something to give. Just as many leaves are used today in medicines and health supplements, so the leaves of the tree of life bring continued physical and spiritual health.

God has prepared a beautiful place for us, just as he prepared a 'very good' environment for Adam and Eve (Genesis 1:31), and he will dwell there with us (21:3). Here, everything is as it should be and trees are right at the centre, nourished by the river of the water of life which flows directly from the throne of God. This is our hope. Let us hold fast to God's promise that one day we will be with him in his holy city.

Heavenly Father, thank you for all that you have provided for us and all that you promise for the future. Make us fit for your kingdom so that we can dwell with you forever. Amen

JACKIE HARRIS

Psalm 119

Caroline Fletcher writes:

We often dip into the book of Psalms to give us a quick burst of encourage-ment. Psalm 119, however, is much longer than the other psalms, so tackling it can feel a bit daunting. This means we may only have skimmed over it or read a few verses from it. We are going to redress that balance by reading Psalm 119 all the way through.

It's best-known verse – 'Your word is a lamp to my feet and a light to my path' (v. 105, NSRV) – sums up the main theme of the psalm – the importance of following in God's ways. This idea is repeated throughout, with different synonyms used for God's word, such as his law, commandments, instruc-tions, ordinances, statutes, decrees and precepts. The psalmist would have been thinking about the laws we find today in our Old Testament. However, as Christians, we also have Jesus' teaching and his Holy Spirit to guide us in how to obey God, so we can think of those things, too, as we take in the message of the psalm.

Psalm 119 is carefully structured, being divided into 22 sections which each contain exactly eight verses. It is a type of acrostic poem based on the 22 letters of the Hebrew alphabet. Unfortunately, it's not obvious from our English translations that the psalmist dedicates each eight-verse section to a different letter of the Hebrew alphabet. Every verse in each of those sec-tions begins with the same Hebrew letter. Some suggest the psalmist meant this as a memory aid to help people meditate and recall different thoughts about obeying God. Others say it is a way of indicating the completeness of God's word: using every letter of the alphabet could symbolise how God's ways are relevant to every aspect of life.

We don't know who wrote the psalm or when it was written. Whoever it was, they were keen to leave us with not only their testimony on the impor-tance of obeying God but also a plethora of examples on how to pray to gain the help and strength we need to be obedient. There is praise, appeal for help, complaint, commitment, confession – prayers to cover every aspect of life. And, as the psalmist's prayers reveal, the writer knew what it was like to serve God in a hostile environment and so has much to teach and encourage us today in our modern world.

Happiness is...

Happy are those whose way is blameless, who walk in the law of the Lord. Happy are those who keep his decrees, who seek him with their whole heart. (NRSV)

Psalm 119 begins with what seems to be a straightforward promise: follow God's laws (God's ways of doing things) and you will be happy. Many translations have 'blessed' instead of happy, but the meaning is similar.

If you were to ask a random selection of people what they need to be happy, I imagine you'd receive a variety of answers! For some it is wrapped up with material wealth and possessions, so happiness for them could be having a new kitchen or the latest phone. Others might say that to be happy requires a problem-free life, without illness, family troubles, stress, etc. This psalm, though, guarantees neither an easy life nor financial rewards. Indeed, later in the psalm we learn that the psalmist was suffering greatly despite his devotion to God's laws. He writes about enduring 'scorn and contempt' from others (v. 22), having his reputation smeared by lies (v. 69) and crying out to God for deliverance from unjust persecution (v. 86).

So, what did the psalmist have in mind by saying following God brings happiness? The New Testament offers some clues. Jesus' teaching known as the beatitudes (Matthew 5:1–12) shows us that Jesus had very different ideas to those around him about what it means to be blessed. He describes those who mourn, the meek and the persecuted as happy. How can this be? The apostle Paul offers us more insight. While imprisoned for preaching the gospel, Paul wrote that he was able to be content despite his bleak circumstances because of the strength God gave him (Philippians 4:11–13). When we walk with God, we too can know deep satisfying happiness, for God goes with us and brings us peace, wisdom, guidance and strength, no matter what we are going through.

Dear Lord, it's easy to be dissatisfied and think that having more 'stuff', money or easier circumstances would bring happiness. Help me to know true contentment, peace and happiness in doing your will and walking with you. Amen
CAROLINE FLETCHER

Not going it alone

I seek you with all my heart; do not let me stray from your commands. (NIV)

On first reading, the psalmist appears very confident in his faith. He declares that he will obey God's decrees and not neglect God's word. However, a closer reading shows he had doubts about his ability to fulfil those promises. He begs God to prevent him straying from his commands (v. 10) and even worries that he may lose his way and be forsaken by God (v. 8).

Like the psalmist, we all know we let God down. Even if we have been Christians a long time and are committed to obeying God, spiteful words can still slip out of our mouths and jealous thoughts infect our minds. The apostle Paul said we all sin and fall short of the glory of God (Romans 3:23). Our attempts to please God are rather like arrows which fail to hit a target: they get so far but just don't make the mark. We cannot reach God's standards in our own strength and the Lord does not expect us to. The psalmist realised this and asked for God's help. We, too, can come to God in our weakness and ask for the power we need to change.

The psalmist may have worried about being rejected by God for failing to keep his commands, but we have one advantage over this Old Testament writer: we know about Jesus and the forgiveness he brings. Remember the beautiful picture of God that Jesus paints in his parable of the prodigal son (Luke 15:11–24)? Christ portrays the Lord as a devoted father longing for his rebellious son to return home. As soon as he spots his son on the horizon, he dashes to meet him and embrace him. Rather than being punished and rejected, the wastrel is welcomed, forgiven and even thrown a party! Thanks be to God for his merciful love.

Spend time reflecting on the ways you fall short in serving and following God. Say sorry to the Lord and then thank him that he forgives you for all those things. Allow time for that truth to really sink in.

CAROLINE FLETCHER

Keeping the faith

Open my eyes that I may see wonderful things in your law. I am a stranger on earth; do not hide your commands from me. (NIV)

As we have already seen, the psalmist had real problems to deal with. Today we learn more about those. Powerful authority figures were actively plotting against him (v. 23). He had some seriously dangerous enemies who had the power to destroy his reputation and ruin his life.

There are several ways he could have reacted to this frightening situation. His devotion to God had made him a target for abuse, perhaps because his enemies were fed up with being made to look bad by his godly behaviour. He could, then, have toned down his devotion to God so that he didn't stand out from the crowd. He could even have joined in with their shady behaviour to try to win their acceptance. The psalmist could also have got angry with God and abandoned his faith completely. After all, his zealous devotion to the Lord seems to have made him unpopular and brought him trouble. It would be easy to feel God had let him down.

But the psalmist reacts in none of these very human ways. Instead, he responds with humility. He likens himself to a 'stranger' in a foreign land (v. 19). Just as a foreigner may struggle to understand the customs, laws and language of an alien country, so the psalmist acknowledges he will struggle to understand God's ways or know why the Lord has allowed bad things to happen to him. Therefore, he asks God to open his eyes, so that he can better understand (v. 18). He pledges to continue devoting himself to God's laws, believing they will guide him in his difficulties (v. 24) and he trusts God to deal with his accusers (v. 22).

How does our faith impact the way we deal with trouble and what can we learn from the psalmist's response to his suffering?

Dear Lord, I am sorry when I struggle to trust you. Help me to understand how to think about and deal with the difficulties I am facing, and give me the strength to keep following in your ways. Amen

CAROLINE FLETCHER

Working with God

I run the way of your commandments, for you enlarge my understanding. (NRSV)

I used to tutor children in literacy and would encourage them to avoid repeating the same words in their writing. However, repetition can be invaluable when you want to emphasise a particular idea, and that is what the psalmist is seeking to do in today's reading. It is not apparent from our English translations, but in the Hebrew, verses 26, 27, 29, 30 and 32 all begin with the same word – 'way'. The psalmist uses it figuratively of the way we lead our lives and repeats it to draw attention to the importance of that way being one of obedience to God.

The psalmist was clearly trying hard to follow God's ways himself (vv. 30–32). However, troubles left him both spiritually and physically exhausted (vv. 25, 28). He knew he needed God to give him the strength and motivation to live the right way and so prayed for God's help (vv. 27, 29, 31). In such times of weakness, we see more clearly what is always true, that obedience to the Lord is something we need to work on – and work on in partnership with God.

Failing to appreciate that leads to two extremes. The first is characterised by leaving everything up to God – thinking that because the Lord forgives us, we don't need to worry about our behaviour. That was an error some of Paul's congregations fell into. Paul had to remind them that they should be trying to lead a Christlike life instead of carrying on in their old ways (Romans 6:1–4). The other extreme is to go it alone – to strive to be better but not realise we need to ask God to help us manage to do this. Are you in danger of either of these extremes?

Spend time confessing any struggles you have obeying God and ask for the strength and motivation to follow in his ways.

CAROLINE FLETCHER

Priorities in prayer

Give me an eagerness for your laws rather than a love for money! Turn my eyes from worthless things, and give me life through your word. (NLT)

What type of things do you pray about? I've just moved house and am praying a lot about all the work that needs doing. It's great to be able to pray about such everyday things, and God wants to hear about all that troubles us. After all, we are told to cast our cares on God because he cares for us (1 Peter 5:7).

However, today's reading reminds me that I should also spend time praying about my spiritual life. The psalmist asks God to teach him his ways and give him understanding so that he can follow God's path instead of chasing material wealth like those around him. How often do we pray like the psalmist?

It is easy to get despondent about our spiritual lives. When it's difficult to motivate ourselves to pray, when reading the Bible is hard work, when going to church feels like a chore to tick off a list, we can become weighed down with guilt and give up trying.

The psalmist, however, offers us hope. He reminds us that God longs to help us with our spiritual lives. The lines in this section of the psalm each begin with a verb. This emphasises that the Lord is a doer, an active God who we can expect to get involved in our lives if we ask him. Prayer gives us access to God's power, so that, no matter how weak and inadequate we may feel, we are never stuck where we are spiritually, for God can help us overcome our flaws. However, we need to be honest with him about our struggles and our failings. There is no point putting on a false front in prayer – God knows us too well for that! It is by being open with the Lord about our weaknesses that we will know his strength.

What are you struggling with in your spiritual life? Share those struggles with God in openness and honesty and ask for his strength to grow stronger in those areas.

CAROLINE FLETCHER

Unbreakable hope

I find my delight in your commandments, because I love them. I revere your commandments, which I love, and I will meditate on your statutes. (NRSV)

In today's reading, the psalmist talks of loving God's commandments (vv. 47–48). This is a strikingly positive way to talk about a set of laws. Why is the psalmist so enthusiastic about them and devoted to observing them despite being taunted for doing so?

He kept them not just because it was the right thing to do, but because doing so brought him hope. He believed that if he kept God's laws, then God would eventually deliver him from his troubles (vv. 41, 45, 49–50, 52, 56).

His belief was based upon the promise, or covenant, God had made to Moses when he gave the Israelites the ten commandments and the other laws in our Old Testament. Moses was told that if the Israelites kept God's laws, they would receive God's blessing and protection. Unfortunately, Old Testament history shows that few were as committed to obeying God as the psalmist. God's people frequently rebelled. Even the psalmist was worried that he might not live up to God's standards (v. 10).

The reality is that we are all let down by our sinful natures. Jesus dealt with this problem by bringing in a new covenant. This covenant offers forgiveness through his death for all who follow him and the gift of the Holy Spirit to help us change from within. So, if the psalmist could find hope in the old covenant which showed people the right way to behave but did not deal with the sin that stopped them following God's ways, then how much more hope can we have in the new covenant which supersedes it? The covenant Jesus brings means our failings are forgiven. If we repent of our sins, they will not stand in the way of God hearing our prayers and helping us in our troubles.

Lord Jesus, thank you so much for loving me enough to die on the cross for me, so that my sins can be forgiven. Thank you that I can know your help and deliverance now, and thank you for your promise of eternal life. Amen

CAROLINE FLETCHER

Motivated by love

When I think of your ways, I turn my feet to your decrees; I hurry and do not delay to keep your commandments. (NRSV)

Characters in soap operas rarely admit their mistakes. They tend to cover up their wrongdoings with more bad choices and dodgy activities until months, or even years, later the truth comes out in one final climactic episode. While such storylines are constructed for dramatic effect, we are all tempted to put off dealing with habits, behaviours and thought patterns that we know are not good. The psalmist, though, was desperate to ensure he was walking in God's ways, so much so that after a time of reflection he describes himself hurrying to change without delay (vv. 59–60).

His unfailing devotion to following God is especially impressive when we consider the troubles he was having. He was surrounded by people who were trying to trip him up and pull him away from God, so what enabled him to be so faithful?

His deep awareness of God's goodness is likely to have been one factor. He talks about waking up at night to praise God. In times of trouble, we often lie awake at night worrying, yet the psalmist used these dark hours to focus on God's goodness and the wisdom of his ways. Similarly, he talks of the earth being full of God's steadfast love. We can lose sight of this when we see all the horrible things going on in the world. Reflecting on the stunning beauty of nature reminds us that God is, indeed, good.

The more we appreciate God's great love for us, the more motivated we are to follow him and get quickly back on to the right path when we stray. This is because our obedience becomes a grateful response to his goodness rather than a reluctant response to guilt. How confident are you of God's steadfast love?

Find a leaf, flower, insect or anything in God's creation to study closely and encourage you in the beauty and wonder of creation and God's goodness. Then, spend time praising the Lord.

CAROLINE FLETCHER

Good out of bad

My suffering was good for me, for it taught me to pay attention to your decrees. (NLT)

In the popular TV programme *The Apprentice*, budding business entrepreneurs compete against each other to win a financial investment and a business partnership with mogul Alan Sugar. The candidates tend to be overconfident characters who exaggerate their success and whitewash their shortcomings. But we all know success is rarely achieved without some errors and wrong turnings along the way. Indeed, our reading reflects this. The psalmist was wholeheartedly committed to God, but even he acknowledges that this was not always so, referring to a time when he went astray (v. 67).

What brought him back? Interestingly, it was not hearing some great teaching or reading an inspiring devotional book, good as those things are. It was a time of affliction that made all the difference. His troubles caused him to see his need for God and turn back to him. This reminds me of the rebellious son in Jesus' parable of the prodigal son, who only came back to his father once he'd hit rock bottom, when he was penniless and feeding pigs (Luke 15:11–32). We can relate to that because we all know how easy it is to forget about God when things are going smoothly, yet how quick we are to turn to prayer in times of trouble.

Looking back on his affliction, the psalmist is even able to declare it to be a good thing (v. 71) because it brought him back to God. This encourages us that even when we fail, even when we let God down, if we turn again to the Lord in our weakness and in repentance, he can use those experiences to help us grow stronger both in our faith and as people. So, let's be honest with ourselves and with the Lord about our shortcomings and let him bring good from our failings.

Are there any times in your life when you remember God bringing good things out of bad situations? Spend time thanking him for the ways you grew both as a person and in your faith through those experiences.

CAROLINE FLETCHER

Grand designs

Your hands have made and fashioned me; give me understanding that I may learn your commandments. (NRSV)

St Augustine famously wrote: 'You have made us for yourself, O Lord, and our hearts are restless until they rest in you' (*Confessions* 1.1.1). In his youth, Augustine led a licentious life, searching for love and meaning in sex, friendships and philosophy. Eventually he came to the realisation that obedience to God was the key to fulfilment.

The psalmist is in similar territory. Today's reading begins with the psalmist's acknowledgment that he was made and fashioned by God, but then he jumps to asking God to help him understand his commandments (v. 73). What is the link between these two seemingly disconnected ideas? As Augustine discovered, because we are made and fashioned by God, it logically follows that we have been designed to live according to his ways and that doing so is what is best for us. Living without God has been described as having 'a God-shaped hole' in our hearts, a sense of emptiness and longing for something more which people often try to satisfy with worldly things like money, success and material possessions.

However, although God has designed us to follow his ways, he hasn't programmed us like robots to automatically obey him without thinking. We have a choice whether to live with him or ignore him. That is why the psalmist jumps from declaring he has been put together by God, to asking God to help him understand his commandments. We need to put in effort to become the people we have been designed to be, especially in this fallen world, which so often pulls us away from God. How much do we believe that we will only find true fulfilment in a life of obedience to God and is that reflected in the amount of effort we put into learning about his ways and following them?

Dear Lord, help us to truly believe that your ways are what are best for us and give us the understanding and strength we need to follow them. Amen
CAROLINE FLETCHER

Be real

My eyes fail with watching for your promise; I ask, 'When will you comfort me?' (NRSV)

Has God ever felt distant? If so, you are in good company. When Mother Teresa's private letters to spiritual confidants were made public after her death, the world was shocked to discover that throughout the long years of her ministry, she had often felt God to be very far away. The psalmist, too, was deeply devoted to God, yet was frustrated at how silent the Lord seemed to him in his troubles.

Unfortunately, we sometimes compound the pain we feel in spiritually dry times with false guilt. We may worry that God feels far away because we have done something wrong, are not spiritual enough or that God does not love us as much as he loves others. The truth is that most people go through times of spiritual dryness and difficulty at some point in their walk with God.

Prayer can be especially difficult in such periods, and it's tempting to give up trying or for our prayer life to simply peter out. The psalmist, however, kept his prayer life going despite his troubles by being brutally honest with the Lord about how he was feeling. Indeed, he uses some vivid imagery to convey his pain, saying his eyes were strained and weary after watching for so long for God to act (v. 82). He also says his sufferings had hurt and damaged him as badly as smoke from a fire disfigures and blackens wineskins (v. 83). He asks God some heart-rending questions as well: 'When will you comfort me?' (v. 82) and 'How long must your servant endure?' (v. 84). If we are going through such times, let's be encouraged that this is a well-trodden path rather than a sign of God's disfavour. And let's not pretend all is well but, like the psalmist, really be honest with God in our prayers.

Spend some time being honest with God about any disappointments, frustrations and pain you feel. If the Lord feels distant, talk to him honestly about that too and, like the psalmist, ask for his comfort.

CAROLINE FLETCHER

Lighting the way

Your word is a lamp to my feet and a light to my path. (NRSV)

I remember once being lost in some woods with my children as it was growing increasingly dark. We were so grateful for the torch on my daughter's phone to see where we were placing our feet, so we could avoid tripping over branches. I was even more grateful when we finally caught sight of a light shining from a distant building which indicated the way out.

Similarly, what the psalmist says about God's word being a light suggests it guides us in both our immediate problems and our more distant goals. His word acts as a lamp shining down around our feet, helping us navigate the daily issues we face at home, work and in society. However, it is also a light that shines forward along a path, guiding us in what our longer-term plans should be.

God's word is clearly very precious, then, keeping us safe from hazards and ensuring we are going the right way. But how do we discover what God is saying to us? Making a commitment to regularly read our Bibles is important. However, as the Bible isn't always easy to understand, we need support with that, so it's important to seek out books, Bible study groups or websites to help us.

We can also hear God speaking to us through prayer. Do we regularly pray about the everyday problems we face and our long-term goals and plans too? Do we also try to leave times of quiet to listen to God's response? The Holy Spirit may speak to us through ideas, thoughts and pictures that pop into our head. It's a good idea to discuss what we have heard with another Christian who can help us test whether those things really are from God.

Spend some time reflecting on steps you can take to grow in your understanding of the Bible. BRF, who publish these notes, have lots of resources to help you in this – their online shop is **brfonline.org.uk**.

CAROLINE FLETCHER

Standing out

It is time for the Lord to act, for your law has been broken. Therefore I love your commandments above gold, above fine gold. (ESV)

We often associate peer pressure with young people. However, that desire to fit in can affect adults too. The phrase 'keeping up with the Joneses' was coined to describe our desire to have what others have and to be like them. We are social beings, so it is not surprising that we find it hard to stand out from the crowd.

The psalmist, however, seems to have spent most of his adult life not fitting in with those around him. It is not obvious in every Bible translation, but in the Hebrew there is a 'therefore' between verses 126 and 127. This connection between the two verses suggests the psalmist is saying that because others are breaking God's law, he will love God's commandments even more, more than gold in fact. Why would the bad behaviour of others drive the psalmist to behave better rather than join in with their godless ways? Perhaps his loyalty to God made him want to compensate for their rebellion. Maybe he was seeking to be an example to his community and draw them back to the Lord.

Certainly, he is an example of being courageous enough to stand out from the crowd and live according to God's principles when others do not. We too are called to not blindly follow everyone else's behaviour. For example, we know we should resist the pressure to join in malicious gossip. However, being prepared to act differently has broader implications too. For instance, do we vote a certain way because our family always has, or do we take the time to consider how a party's policies align with God's priorities? What aspects of modern life might God want us to challenge rather than simply go along with the views of those around us?

Dear Lord, help me not to be apathetic about issues like injustice, poverty and the environment. Please show me how I can be an example to others and stand up for your values. Amen

CAROLINE FLETCHER

Praying through the day

I rise before dawn and cry for help; I put my hope in your words. My eyes are awake before each watch of the night, that I may meditate on your promise. (NRSV)

When I had my first baby, my prayer routine collapsed. I used to have a regular morning quiet time, when I would pray and read my Bible away from noise and distraction. But with a baby that became impossible! She'd start crying and want comforting, feeding or her nappy changed. Even if I did get space to pray, I'd soon fall asleep after all the broken nights. I felt guilty that my prayers consisted of short sentences scattered across the day rather than the focused time I'd enjoyed previously.

The psalmist's prayer life reminds us that there are different patterns of prayer. He would have followed the Jewish practice of praying three times a day, and we read about him here praying in the early hours of the morning and at night (vv. 147–148). Our modern work patterns and commitments will prevent most of us from copying him, but his words act as a reminder that prayer is not limited to one time of day. Indeed, I finally got over my guilt about my prayer life when I realised that the short prayers I managed to say when pushing the pram or cleaning were just as valid and important as the longer prayers that I'd had time for before children.

In fact, praying short little prayers throughout the day is a good discipline, for it reminds us that God is always with us in the busyness of life as well as in the quiet times. The psalmist took comfort from this truth. He describes his enemies as near, but he did not lose hope because he knew God was near too (vv. 150–151). Praying throughout the day helps us to become more conscious of the presence of God, which is with us wherever we are, whatever we are doing and whatever we face.

Whenever you begin to worry today or think about a problem you or someone else is facing, try sending up an arrow prayer – a short little prayer asking God to help with those issues.

CAROLINE FLETCHER

Praise is powerful

Powerful people harass me without cause, but my heart trembles only at your word. I rejoice in your word like one who discovers a great treasure. (NLT)

Many of us will be familiar with the old hymn 'Great is thy faithfulness'. What we may not know is that this hymn was inspired by verses from the Old Testament book Lamentations. As its name suggests, Lamentations is a book of mourning. It describes the destruction of Jerusalem, which had been razed to the ground by the Babylonian army. However, it also contains these beautiful words of praise which inspired the hymn: 'The steadfast love of the Lord never ceases, his mercies never come to an end; they are new every morning; great is your faithfulness' (Lamentations 3:22–23, NRSV). The author of Lamentations was heartbroken, but he still trusted that God was at work in his people's suffering.

As we have seen before, the psalmist was also suffering. He talks about having many enemies who persecute him and asks God to save him (vv. 156–157). Yet despite his suffering, he still manages to keep on praising God. He talks about rejoicing in God's word as someone rejoices after finding great treasure (v. 162). He even says he praises God seven times a day (v. 164), which is probably a way of saying he did so frequently throughout the day.

We know it is right to praise God in all circumstances: scripture encourages us in this. But praising God when times are hard is not just something we do for God; it benefits us too. It lifts our eyes from the apparent hopelessness of our situation and reminds us that God is bigger than our problems. It encourages us that God is good, powerful and just, and it builds up our faith, helping us to trust God despite our pain, doubts and questions. Do we praise God when things are tough or only when everything is going well?

Dear Lord, thank you that no matter what is going on in my life and no matter how dark things may seem, I can always praise you, for you have my life in your hands and you love me. Amen

CAROLINE FLETCHER

God's gift of grace

Victoria Byrne writes:

Grace is a beautifully big topic. I have been noticing how the idea saturates so many passages in the New Testament. God's grace is the defining feature of the Christian religion. It encompasses the forgiveness, blessings and freedom from sin that he offers his penitent people. Grace is at the heart of the good news, for God does not treat us as we deserve but offers us new life through Christ: 'The old has gone, the new is here!' (2 Corinthians 5:17, NIV).

In graciously offering us freedom from our past, God does not want us to be automatons. He does not want us limited and programmed, afraid to take risks, anxiously maintaining good behaviour, trying to keep our heads down or narrowly obeying the rules out of fear of his judgement. We are encouraged to flourish within a relationship of trust, as children of a good Father, and where we know that mistakes can be put behind us. I have heard people say that they are not good enough for church. That fear of not living up to God's expectations is a tragic misunderstanding of what God really offers.

While God's grace is perfect, humans are not; sometimes we hurt people by not being gracious to each other. The gospels show that Jesus understood our human frailties. He was always ready to offer people acceptance, kindness, truth and a way forward. He modelled how to be a flourishing human and was gentle with those who stumbled.

Even as Christians, we might understand grace as a concept, but we are often still learning what grace really means for us. Meanwhile, we can all too easily be tempted to try earning our way into God's good books. In truth, when we became Christians, our name was written into the book of life. However hard our lives are, his grace opens the way for us to experience the depth and richness of a relationship with God our maker, or our Father, as Jesus called him. Good behaviour is something that will naturally grow from loving Jesus and living out grace because we want to please the God of love and life.

God has been the engine of joy, freedom and good relationships in my life. My hope is that as we journey together in the coming twelve days, we will see grace at work in ordinary human relationships as well as in the extraordinary generosity of God.

Saved by grace

There was only one possible way for God to give away his righteousness and still be true to both his justice and his mercy – to offer up his own Son. So now, because we stand on the faithfulness of Jesus, God declares us righteous in his eyes! (TPT)

I have been enjoying reading God's word in The Passion translation. After years of Bible study, it's refreshing to hear familiar ideas expressed in a new way. I feel I need that, especially for this central truth of the gospel, that salvation comes from God, which is God's greatest act of grace to us.

I wonder if the disciples and Paul often felt similarly enlivened as Jesus reinterpreted familiar passages of the Torah in the light of the new covenant. Our passage today is a big-picture account of God's grace to humanity. I was struck by the words 'to offer up his own Son'. It reminded me of Abraham's willingness to sacrifice his son Isaac (Genesis 22:1–10). Both are shocking. For Abraham, as for Jesus, success meant doing God's will, whatever it was. This epistle was written to churches in Rome, who lived at the heart of an empire of worldly success. These verses remind us that salvation was earned for us by God's humility, suffering and love. It's not something we've earned or simply a nice benefit of our faith.

Jesus the Messiah chose to stoop low and suffer, because he trusted the loving heart of the Father. By choosing to align ourselves with, and commit ourselves to, Jesus, we accept that we need God's rescue. He generously exchanges our sin for his divine righteousness. The generosity of God is hard to understand and sometimes it makes me feel uncomfortable; but God knows I could not save myself, and I underestimate how much he loves me and wants to be profoundly united with me. Jesus was committed to submitting his life to the Father on every level, and I'm feeling challenged to be 'all-in' too.

God declares believers righteous and at one with God. You may like to meditate on the nature of God, with whom you are at one.

VICTORIA BYRNE

Grace, the expression of love

He does not treat us as our sins deserve or repay us according to our iniquities… As a father has compassion on his children, so the Lord has compassion on those who fear him; for he knows how we are formed. (NIV)

God's grace is the visible flowering of his great mercy towards us. It overlooks our ignorance and imperfections and extends love to us anyway. He created us for life, and he's doing all he can to make sure we can live it to the full. We often get ourselves into tangles and prisons of our own making and do not deserve God's mercy, but it is God's gift. Jesus died as the ultimate unpicking of the lock.

Setting out on this study, I was overawed by our topic. It is so central to the workings of the whole of our faith. Theologians write reams about grace, salvation and redemption; and they can get very technical about how grace operates, its functions, its timings and underpinning mechanisms.

I recall the time soon after my own reawakening to God's grace, when I was doing Bible studies with a church student worker and discovering God's forgiveness, love and merciful kindness towards me. While the technicalities of how God's grace relates to me are vital to understand, that theological understanding didn't affect me nearly as much as the way people treated me while they shared with me about God.

In the years since then, I've learnt so much both from the scriptures and God's people, but most readily from the way grace is modelled to me by fellow believers. In fact, I recall it being the student worker's manner and tone towards me as much as any clever thing she said that won me over back in 1990. How she treated me was consistent with what we were reading in John 17, where Jesus' beautiful attitudes and thoughts were on display.

Those who love me are the ones who remind me that God is gracious and compassionate. Their love and forgiveness help set me free.

How have people demonstrated grace to you and what impact did that have? How might you share God's grace with others?

VICTORIA BYRNE

A graceful posture

Many are saying of me, 'God will not deliver him.' But you, Lord, are a shield around me, my glory, the One who lifts my head high. (NIV)

I have been thinking about the way we describe people as graceful, and often that means physical grace. There's an implication of naturally good posture and someone who moves with ease. I recently experienced the connection between God's grace and an improvement in my own physical posture.

My friend had prayed for me and sensed God's good, affirming plans for me, over which I had harboured self-doubts. Filled with fresh hope, I found myself sitting more upright and holding my head high. I had been unaware of previously sitting with hunched shoulders, but it suddenly felt uncomfortable to sit that way. Trusting God's grace made me see myself differently.

Physical ease is not always related to a gracious attitude. Through my work as a seniors' pastor, I've known several remarkable people in their 80s and 90s who have had nothing but a kind and gracious attitude towards others, despite living with physical frustrations and even chronic pain. What have they in common? They have a consistent determination to stay close to Jesus, to seek out his presence and to keep reading the scriptures. They face challenges in collaboration with God and seek to be a blessing to others. When we talk, they refer to God as much as anyone else. He is their primary caregiver.

Jesus himself displayed divine grace under pressure of all kinds during his ministry. Even on the cross, he looked to the needs of others and forgave those who would not accept him. This challenges me. Am I really gracious towards others, or do I just want to look as if nothing's wrong? What does my posture reveal about how I am really feeling?

What physical postures do you find yourself adopting in prayer and at other times? Bring to God any feelings of self-doubt or resentment and ask him to enable you to lift your head high.

VICTORIA BYRNE

The God of all grace

And the God of all grace, who called you to his eternal glory in Christ, after you have suffered a little while, will himself restore you and make you strong, firm and steadfast. To him be the power forever and ever. Amen. (NIV)

I went for a walk very early this morning when the streets were empty. The sun was already very bright, making the river sparkle. It was a relief and a joy after a gloomy season.

This beautiful phrase, 'the God of all grace', was rolling around my thoughts the whole time. Why does this description resound so well? Perhaps because there is something inherently generous about sunshine and grace. Not just God of 'grace', but of 'all grace', grace abundantly poured out beyond measure – an overflowing cup. A 'grace period' goes beyond the strict requirements of a contract; by grace, God will restore us in ways we could not earn or expect.

We need to connect with the God of all grace, especially when the world's news headlines are hard-hitting. Peter's word reminds me to refocus on the conviction that God will restore (in this life and the next) those who believe; he will answer every prayer. His grace is abundant, generous and can heal our broken world. We recall scripture's reassurances: 'He will wipe every tear from their eyes' (Revelation 21:4). In his letter, Peter was addressing people who needed to stand firm in the face of an attack on God's truth. That 'little while' of suffering is an understatement, and we all know it can be a fight to keep the faith. But Peter is also reminding us that in comparison with the joy of experiencing heaven's vivid, ongoing revelation of God, this will seem like a 'little while'.

I came home from my walk and found today's verse echoed in a global call to prayer. I felt both encouraged and thankful that, while there is so much to pray for, we can call upon the God of all grace.

A prompt for prayer today: 'I will tell of the kindnesses of the Lord, the deeds for which he is to be praised, according to all the Lord has done for us' (Isaiah 63:7).

VICTORIA BYRNE

My heart is filled with thankfulness
To Him who bore my pain;
Who plumbed the depths of my disgrace
And gave me life again.
Who crushed my curse of sinfulness,
And clothed me with His light,
And wrote His law of righteousness
With power upon my heart.

My heart is filled with thankfulness
To Him who walks beside;
Who floods my weaknesses with strength
And causes fears to fly;
Whose every promise is enough
For every step I take,
Sustaining me with arms of love
And crowning me with grace.

My heart is filled with thankfulness
To Him who reigns above;
Whose wisdom is my perfect peace,
Whose every thought is love.
For every day I have on earth
Is given by the King.
So I will give my life, my all,
To love and follow Him.

Stuart Townend & Keith Getty
Copyright © 2004 Thankyou Music

Being in the flow of God's grace

But he continues to pour out more and more grace upon us. For it says, 'God resists you when you are proud but continually pours out grace when you are humble.' (TPT)

I saw a moving video on *BBC News* today. A national politician in Ukraine was in St Sophia Cathedral in Kyiv. Clive Myrie, the reporter, noted they were seeking 'divine guidance', and I recalled that 'Sophia' means 'wisdom'. Any time we seek God's thoughts, we are acknowledging that his ways are not our ways and that we want to lean on his understanding.

It's easy to judge good and evil in the global headlines; harder to acknowledge when I might be on the wrong path myself and need God to correct my route. This can be as true in small matters as in great ones. This past week at work, I have been challenged at the prospect of phoning someone who had expressed a great deal of anger at my colleague and potentially had a complaint against me. I was naturally upset by this and, despite a desire to focus on finding out the details of the problem and try to help, I realised that I was avoiding making the phone call, guided only by my fear of criticism.

It took me days to hear God's compassionate heart for this person and, even then, I could only contact her as an act of pure obedience. After much preparation and prayer, I managed to put aside my fears of her strong emotional response and put her needs before my own. The call went well and what had seemed at first to be a complaint was revealed to be a cry for help. This person was clearly in a lot of emotional pain. I realised that God had been speaking clearly during my preparation, when he said, 'Listen to her. Be patient, kind and long-suffering. It's not about you.'

Is there a situation that you are struggling with today? Bring it to God, asking for his guidance and grace to enable you to move forward.

VICTORIA BYRNE

Our gracious host

'They will condemn him to death and will hand him over to the Gentiles, who will mock him and spit on him, flog him and kill him. Three days later he will rise.' (NIV)

I have been thinking of the wider ways we see grace at work in daily life and, in doing so, I am struck by the expansive idea of grace. When I recall actions that display God's grace, their description seems to overflow neat boundaries. A gracious host comes to mind, who was unselfishly considerate of her guests and gave us a beautiful time. But the graciousness of her hosting also meant people felt safe, and in that atmosphere, we had wonderful conversation. The more I think about the word grace, it expands into a beautiful symphony of related actions and consequences.

I note that our word grace comes from the Latin *gratia*, meaning pleasing, thankful. So, if we want to imagine what grace looks like, we could ask ourselves what has made us thankful.

I sense that someone acting graciously knows they have something to give and gives generously. We cannot give graciously if we fear we lack the resources to be able to give something away. The gracious person is secure enough (be that materially, emotionally, spiritually) to reach out to others and to help meet their needs, in whatever way that seems appropriate.

In this passage, we see the full extent of the graciousness of Jesus. He was able to undergo the terrible suffering of crucifixion because his security was in God the Father. He was able to die for us because he trusted in the Father's plan to rescue humanity. Jesus told his disciples: 'I came from the Father and entered the world; now I am leaving the world and going back to the Father' (John 16:28). By God's grace, his Son had the strength to follow the Father's will. By God's generosity, we are raised with Jesus too.

In what ways has God been gracious to you recently, and what fruit is that producing?

VICTORIA BYRNE

Growing in grace

And the child grew and became strong; he was filled with wisdom, and the grace of God was on him. (NIV)

People love to talk about potential, but sometimes this can be a source of stress. We can feel pressure to live up to someone else's expectations of our life (as individuals or groups). Scripture tells us that God has bestowed on us more resources and opportunities than we can ever fully explore, and sometimes this too feels like a heavy thing to carry. But this is to forget God's grace.

Jesus fulfilled God's potential for him as he grew. Luke tells us that Jesus 'grew in wisdom and stature, and in favour with God and man' (2:52). I find it thought provoking that the young Jesus, though sinless, could grow in these areas.

I was interested to discover that the word for 'growth' used in this verse originally referred to advancing, in the sense of cutting down trees to settle in what was once forest. This reminded me of the Israelites surveying the enormity of the land of milk and honey that they were supposed to go in and possess (Deuteronomy 1:8). The obstacles looked so big, and fear held them back. We need to trust in God's grace as we look out over the land of God-given opportunity ahead of us. We surely need God's help to see how we might fulfil his purposes. As I reflect on my life, I see how God has enabled me to advance: growing my understanding and strength to explore and develop all that he has prepared for me.

And this growth continues throughout our lives. Anna, the prophetess in this passage, spent a lifetime preparing for her key moment of purpose: meeting and prophesying over Jesus the Messiah in her 80s.

'He who began a good work in you will carry it on to completion until the day of Christ Jesus' (Philippians 1:6).

VICTORIA BYRNE

God's strength in us

But he said to me, 'My grace is sufficient for you, for my power is made perfect in weakness.' Therefore I will boast all the more gladly about my weaknesses, so that Christ's power may rest on me. (NIV)

In my work as a church ministry leader, I frequently speak in front of a roomful of people or work with my team to lead services, taking responsibility for the tone and content of a meeting. In doing so, we have many chances to acknowledge our need for God's grace. We cannot manufacture spiritual encounters: we need God to reveal himself. Without his presence, our work means little.

I am often surprised at how fully God answers our cry for help. Perhaps a talk connects with the congregation more than I expect or God's presence is clear as we pray together about something overwhelming. I'm learning that my request for help doesn't work if I only go through the motions of asking for his help and strength. I need to come to the king of kings in real humility, acknowledging my empty-handedness.

I am even more aware of my need for God's strength when I'm doing something brave like giving a talk on a day when I'm feeling particularly inadequate. Then I'm glad to remember what Matthew 5:6 tells us, 'Blessed are those who hunger and thirst…' I need God because I am mortal and do not love as he loves; I have limited courage, capacity and faith. But I can trust that I am to bring the 'two loaves and fish' and he will bring the multiplication. On those days of weakness, I learn that even on the good days, it is not me who makes good things happen, but him.

The irony is that the people you see being used most powerfully by God are probably most in need of encouragement and prayer. They are living at the boundary of their knowledge and strength, right out on the edge of their comfort zone.

Try giving thanks or encouragement this week to someone who might outwardly seem like they don't need it.

VICTORIA BYRNE

God's grace equips us to obey him

Lord, you alone are my portion and my cup; you make my lot secure...
I will praise the Lord, who counsels me; even at night my heart
instructs me. I keep my eyes always on the Lord. With him at my right
hand, I will not be shaken. (NIV)

God's unearned grace equips us to serve him with healthy motives. I have
been wanting to serve on a particular team at church for a long time, but the
opening never seemed to come. When I pushed, I was pushed back; when
I didn't push, I just felt frustrated. I wonder if you have ever felt the same.

Today, during a church meeting, my colleague reminded us of God's grace,
by which we are not chiefly people busily obeying God, but God's dearly
beloved children. We are his because he first loved us. We had a time of
quiet prayer so we could let God sink those truths deeper into us. I distinctly
sensed the Spirit engaging directly with me, and I asked him why the thing
I thought he was calling me into never seemed to happen. Was I wrong? I
believe he showed me a great truth when he responded: 'If this isn't right
(indicating himself and me), then that won't help.'

Shortly afterwards, I was asked to join the team I had wanted to join!
By God's grace I hope that I continue serving with the same firm conviction
that any role I hold is not the centre of my relationship with God. It's never
about what I do.

In God's eyes we are all jewels for the display of his splendour, empowered by his grace to do the works he planned in advance for us, through
our many different gifts and callings. Whether I feel elated or challenged
by the things he wants me to do, the quality of my connection with him is
what determines my spiritual health.

If you stopped (or started) serving God in a particular way tomorrow, what
would God think? Ask him!

VICTORIA BYRNE

Provision in the moment

'On my account you will be brought before governors and kings as witnesses to them and to the Gentiles. But when they arrest you, do not worry about what to say or how to say it. At that time you will be given what to say.' (NIV)

God gave us Jesus because we were powerless to help ourselves (Romans 5:6). His grace rescues us in the most fundamental way. But it also shows up in countless daily ways, both big and small.

This week I noticed myself spontaneously saying something wise, in a way that felt heaven-sent, blessing me and those around me. It was a gift of grace for the moment. It happened during a meeting, when I was suddenly asked to summarise how leading a service brings me enjoyment.

In fact, I had been rather wrestling with the self-consciousness of being up front leading a service. I had wanted to quell old fears that I'm just seeking attention when I take the lead. And yet I feel real joy when I lead a church service: it is a genuine partnership with God.

When I was put on the spot in the meeting, I had a moment of profound clarity. I realised that I love leading services because I can put words to what we are experiencing together and serve the group by voicing thoughts that we all share. Doing so breaks down walls between our individual experiences of God and our collective experiences as a congregation.

When this understanding came to me it felt like a gift, a small example of God's grace, delivered to me unbidden. God gave me a new, healthy way to think about leading from the front of church that I didn't know I needed. God had always empowered me on past occasions, and I can trust him to do that in the future.

Father, thank you that you are always ready to meet with us. Help us to see your grace at work in our lives today. Amen

VICTORIA BYRNE

The effect of receiving grace

Christ died for our sins… [I] do not even deserve to be called an apostle, because I persecuted the church of God. But by the grace of God I am what I am, and his grace to me was not without effect. (NIV)

I'm not sure we will ever get to a point where we feel that we have fully explored God's grace in this life. I know that as the years go by, I grow more grateful for God's willingness to overcome my failings and forgive my sins.

In my work as a seniors' ministry leader, I get to study the Bible regularly with people nearly twice my age. They have lived long lives and they are still learning, still humble, still grateful to God. I love talking with them about God and their experiences of life as we study his word together. They are aware that God's work in them is still ongoing. Though they have gained much wisdom in their maturity, their willingness to keep on learning reassures me that there is always more of God's grace to discover. As we 'live and learn' we make mistakes, but we never exhaust God's grace.

The people of my acquaintance who have travelled with God the longest are the most aware of being in receipt of God's undeserved favour – his grace. They do that by noticing it, being thankful for it and trusting God at his word. By turn, they gladly extend grace to others.

In his letters, the apostle Paul regularly shows his undying gratitude to God. He never forgets how he persecuted Jesus, frequently refers to his awareness of God's grace for him and humbly calls himself the 'least of the apostles'. God's gift of grace in forgiving him powered Paul's whole ministry. Christ died for each of us too, to free us from our sins and to give us eternal life. May I always be alive to that.

'Praise be to the God and Father of… Jesus Christ! In his great mercy he has given us new birth into a living hope through the resurrection of Jesus Christ… into an inheritance that can never perish, spoil or fade' (1 Peter 1:3–4).

VICTORIA BYRNE

Grace: unfair but wonderful

God, who is rich in mercy, made us alive with Christ even when we were dead in transgressions – it is by grace you have been saved. And God raised us up with Christ and seated us with him in the heavenly realms in Christ Jesus. (NIV)

God's grace – God's Reward At Christ's Expense – is difficult for us to grasp, because it is entirely undeserved. How do we make sense of God's gift of his presence: guaranteed, secure, from-now-on-for-the-rest-of-time; life suffused with God's infinite glory in return for only our saying 'yes' to Jesus and following him. It doesn't add up. It can offend our sense of fairness. Yet, Jesus sacrificed his own life to make this possible.

I have been writing for *Day by Day with God* for a few years now. It takes months to wrangle the ideas into words and redraft them until they form all the right sentences. I wonder if it ever looks like I have life as a Christian all worked out! As I have worked on these notes, I realise that I have barely scratched the surface on this topic of God's grace. I suspect that in this life we only ever glimpse a fraction of how big God's grace is.

A friend praying for me today sensed God promising a breakthrough in our ministry. This is God's grace at work. Whether we find ourselves in a 'winter' or 'harvest' season in our ministry, it's never really a direct line to what we have put into it; we can't outgive God. Our success isn't earned; the work in people's hearts is God's ministry and any victory just shows his grace towards those we serve.

The Bible is overflowing with extraordinary promises for those who align themselves with Christ. It's easy sometimes to read them without fully appreciating what they tell us. Too often, we underestimate the goodness of God. He is scandalously liberal with his gifts! Each of us has been offered an extraordinary exchange: our old, cast-off, misshapen garments for his heavenly glory. What extraordinary grace!

'So Jesus said to the Jews who had believed him, "If you abide in my word, you are truly my disciples, and you will know the truth, and the truth will set you free"' (John 8:31–32, ESV). Ponder these words and respond in prayer.

VICTORIA BYRNE

Enabling all ages to grow in faith

Anna Chaplaincy

Living Faith

Messy Church

Parenting for Faith

BRF is a Christian charity that resources individuals and
churches. Our vision is to enable people of all ages to grow in
faith and understanding of the Bible and to see more people
equipped to exercise their gifts in leadership and ministry.

To find out more about our work, visit

brf.org.uk

Recommended reading

World Turned Upside Down
The Psalms and the spirituality of pain – finding a way through
Alison Morgan
978 1 80039 166 6 £12.99
brfonline.org.uk

When we are at our weakest, when we feel we most need God and yet have no idea how to talk to him, it is the Psalms which leap to our rescue. With the psalmists as our guides, we learn to draw closer to God, to hear his voice in fresh ways, and to identify what it is that troubles us. Borrowing their words, we find that we are able to articulate our most painful feelings and walk through suffering with honesty, hope, and confidence in the God who travels beside us. Here is an opportunity to read the Psalms differently: an invitation to embark on a new journey.

This Crown of Comfort
God's seven calls to women in distress
Eva Leaf
978 1 80039 208 3 £9.99
brfonline.org.uk

God deeply cares for those of us who are broken and hurt. And just as he helped his beloved Jerusalem find healing in her brokenness, he does the same for us. For he cried out seven double imperatives to her in the book of Isaiah, seven steps to restore her to wholeness, and he cries out the same to us. But he doesn't begin by scolding us; instead, he comforts. His first double imperative is, 'Comfort, comfort,' despite what has happened in our lives. In *This Crown of Comfort*, Eva Leaf shares stories from her own life and from the lives of other women of how God met them in their brokenness.

To order

Online: **brfonline.org.uk**
Telephone: +44 (0)1865 319700
Mon–Fri 9.30–17.00

Delivery times within the UK are normally 15 working days. Prices are correct at the time of going to press but may change without prior notice.

Title	Price	Qty	Total
World Turned Upside Down	£12.99		
This Crown of Comfort	£9.99		

POSTAGE AND PACKING CHARGES			
Order value	UK	Europe	Rest of world
Under £7.00	£2.00		
£7.00–£29.99	£3.00	Available on request	Available on request
£30.00 and over	FREE		

Total value of books	
Donation	
Postage and packing	
Total for this order	

Please complete in BLOCK CAPITALS

Title _____ First name/initials _____ Surname _____

Address _____

_____ Postcode _____

Acc. No. _____ Telephone _____

Email _____

Method of payment

☐ Cheque (made payable to BRF) ☐ MasterCard / Visa

Card no. ▯▯▯▯ ▯▯▯▯ ▯▯▯▯ ▯▯▯▯ ▯▯▯▯ ▯▯▯▯

Expires end ▯▯ M M ▯▯ Y Y Security code ▯▯▯ Last 3 digits on the reverse of the card

Registered with FUNDRAISING REGULATOR

Please return this form to:
BRF, 15 The Chambers, Vineyard, Abingdon OX14 3FE | enquiries@brf.org.uk

For terms and cancellation information, please visit **brfonline.org.uk/terms**.

SUBSCRIPTION INFORMATION

Each issue of *Day by Day with God* is available from Christian bookshops everywhere. Copies may also be available through your church book agent or from the person who distributes Bible reading notes in your church.

Alternatively you may obtain *Day by Day with God* on subscription direct from the publishers. There are two kinds of subscription:

Individual subscriptions
covering 3 issues for 4 copies or less, payable in advance
(including postage & packing).

To order, please complete the details on page 144 and return with the appropriate payment to: BRF, 15 The Chambers, Vineyard, Abingdon OX14 3FE

You can also use the form on page 144 to order a gift subscription for a friend.

Group subscriptions
covering 3 issues for 5 copies or more, sent to one UK address (post free).

Please note that the annual billing period for group subscriptions runs from 1 May to 30 April.

To order, please complete the details on page 143 and return with the appropriate payment to: BRF, 15 The Chambers, Vineyard, Abingdon OX14 3FE

You will receive an invoice with the first issue of notes.

All our Bible reading notes can be ordered online by visiting
brfonline.org.uk/collections/subscriptions

Day by Day with God is also available as
an app for Android, iPhone and iPad
brfonline.org.uk/collections/apps

All subscription enquiries should be directed to:
BRF, 15 The Chambers, Vineyard, Abingdon OX14 3FE
+44 (0)1865 319700 | **enquiries@brf.org.uk**

DBDWG0223

DAY BY DAY WITH GOD GROUP SUBSCRIPTION FORM

> All our Bible reading notes can be ordered online by visiting
> **brfonline.org.uk/collections/subscriptions**

The group subscription rate for *Day by Day with God* will be £14.85 per person until April 2024.

☐ I would like to take out a group subscription for _____ (quantity) copies.

☐ Please start my order with the September 2023 / January 2024 / May 2024* issue. I would like to pay annually/receive an invoice* with each edition of the notes. (*delete as appropriate)

Please do not send any money with your order. Send your order to BRF and we will send you an invoice.

Name and address of the person organising the group subscription:

Title _____ First name/initials _____ Surname _____

Address_____

_____ Postcode _____

Telephone _____ Email _____

Church_____

Name and address of the person paying the invoice if the invoice needs to be sent directly to them:

Title _____ First name/initials _____ Surname _____

Address_____

_____ Postcode _____

Telephone _____ Email _____

We will use your personal data to process this order. From time to time we may send you information about the work of BRF. Please contact us if you wish to discuss your mailing preferences **brf.org.uk/privacy**

Please return this form to:
BRF, 15 The Chambers, Vineyard, Abingdon OX14 3FE | **enquiries@brf.org.uk**
For terms and cancellation information, please visit **brfonline.org.uk/terms**.

Bible Reading Fellowship is a charity (233280) and company limited by guarantee (301324), registered in England and Wales

DAY BY DAY WITH GOD INDIVIDUAL/GIFT SUBSCRIPTION FORM

> To order online, please visit **brfonline.org.uk/collections/subscriptions**

☐ I would like to give a gift subscription (please provide both names and addresses)

☐ I would like to take out a subscription myself (complete your name and address details only once)

Title _____ First name/initials _____ Surname _____

Address _____

_____ Postcode _____

Telephone _____ Email _____

Gift subscription name _____

Gift subscription address _____

_____ Postcode _____

Gift subscription (20 words max. or include your own gift card):

_____

_____

Please send *Day by Day with God* beginning with the September 2023 / January 2024 / May 2024 issue (*delete as appropriate*):

(*please tick box*)	UK	Europe	Rest of world
1-year subscription	☐ £19.05	☐ £26.55	☐ £30.45
2-year subscription	☐ £36.30	N/A	N/A

Optional donation to support the work of BRF £ _____

Total enclosed £ _____ (cheques should be made payable to 'BRF')

Please charge my MasterCard / Visa with £ _____

Card no. ☐☐☐☐ ☐☐☐☐ ☐☐☐☐ ☐☐☐☐

Expires end ☐M☐M ☐Y☐Y   Security code ☐☐☐   Last 3 digits on the reverse of the card

We will use your personal data to process this order. From time to time we may send you information about the work of BRF. Please contact us if you wish to discuss your mailing preferences **brf.org.uk/privacy**

Please return this form to:

BRF, 15 The Chambers, Vineyard, Abingdon OX14 3FE | **enquiries@brf.org.uk**

For terms and cancellation information, please visit **brfonline.org.uk/terms**.

Bible Reading Fellowship is a charity (233280) and company limited by guarantee (301324), registered in England and Wales

DBDWG0223